P9-CKF-468

WOOD® MAGAZINE

SCROLLSAW Patterns

STERLING PUBLISHING CO. INC., NEW YORK

Wood Magazine Scrollsaw Patterns

ACKNOWLEDGMENTS

A great deal of appreciation is due to the past and present design and editorial staff of Meredith Corporation's *Better Homes & Gardens*® *WOOD*® magazine for many of the patterns, projects, and technical advice presented in this book. Individual scrollsawyers also contributed their designs, and they're noted on page 192. A special thanks is due to Rick Hutcheson, a prolific professional scroller whose savvy of the craft appears endless. Thanks, also, to the tips and tricks provided by fretwork hobbyist Carl Weckhorst, and skilled scrollsaw craftsmen Roy King and Scott Kochendorfer. And finally, much gratitude to Administrative Assistant Sheryl Munyon at *WOOD*® magazine, Jackie Keuck, Meredith's art library manager, and Cheryl Cibula for their efforts in helping me assemble all the material that appears within these pages.

Peter J. Stephano

Library of Congress Cataloging-in-Publication Data

Wood magazine scroll saw patterns.

    p. cm.

  Includes index.

  ISBN 1-4027-0750-9

  1. Jig saws. 2. Woodwork--Patterns. I. Title: Scrollsaw patterns. II.

Better homes and gardens wood.

TT186.W63 2004

745.51'3--dc22

2004006725

Published by Sterling Publishing Co., Inc.

387 Park Avenue South, New York, NY 10016

© 2005 by *Wood*® magazine

This edition is based on material that has been featured in Wood® Magazine

Distributed in Canada by Sterling Publishing

⁒ Canadian Manda Group, 165 Dufferin Street

Toronto, Ontario, Canada M6K 3H6

Distributed in Great Britain by Chrysalis Books Group PLC

The Chrysalis Building, Bramley Road, London W10 6SP, England

Distributed in Australia by Capricorn Link (Australia) Pty. Ltd.

P.O. Box 704, Windsor, NSW 2756, Australia

Printed in China

Sterling ISBN 1-4027-0750-9

CONTENTS

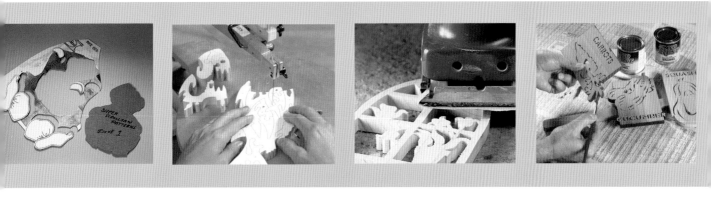

INTRODUCTION

The majority of scrollsawyers are like most woodworkers and other people who enjoy making things with their hands: They have the production skills, but not the ability to come up with totally original designs. That's why in the crafts field you find plans available for furniture of all types, and patterns for everything from needlework to rosemaling. There's nothing wrong with working from a plan or pattern. Nearly everyone requires a starting place— so consider this book of scrollsaw patterns to be yours.

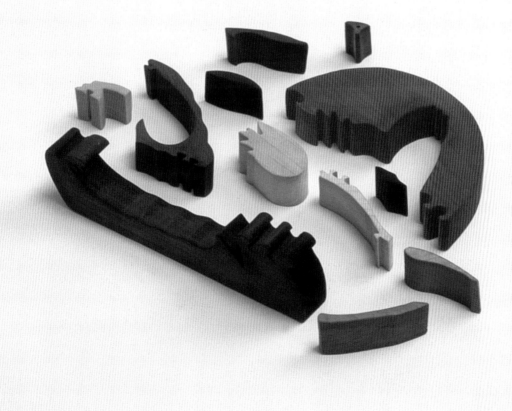

On the following pages you'll discover patterns for animals and autos, birds and buildings, people and places—just about anything imaginable. Using them, you can make the projects shown, usually quite easily. Remember, though, the provided patterns are yours to use as you may. You can incorporate the pattern associated with one project into an entirely different one. Or, as many scrollsawyers do, you may use a particularly appealing part of a pattern and apply it to a box or other project. This is where your own creativity comes into play.

With few exceptions, the patterns you'll find on the following pages are presented in full size. However, there's no rule that says you must utilize them that way. Today, most photocopy machines have the ability to enlarge as well as reduce. It's only a matter of selecting the desired enlarging or reducing percentage (within the limits), placing the pattern on the glass, and pushing a button. And due to demand as well as lower prices, photocopiers aren't limited to the office anymore. You'll find them selling for well under $200—an affordable price for the home if you plan to do a lot of pattern copying. For limited use at a reasonable per copy cost, there are also machines located in such places as supermarkets, libraries, and printing/copying centers.

Pelican puzzle that appears in Chapter 9. The pattern can be found on page 174.

1

Getting Started Scrolling

MAKING PATTERNS STICK

Most professional scrollsawyers and serious hobbyists prefer to adhere a paper pattern to the workpiece (the wood or other material) with spray adhesive or rubber cement—both available at office and art supply stores—rather than draw or trace it on. This results in better visibility of the pattern lines. Some scrollers always turn to spray adhesive because they find that the rubber cement on very large patterns dries too quickly and the pattern lifts up before they've finished cutting. This isn't a problem with spray adhesive, and the pattern comes off easily with lacquer thinner or lighter fluid.

On the other hand, other scrollsawyers believe that nothing tops rubber cement for sticking on paper patterns because it's cheap, fast, holds the pattern firmly, goes on without the hassle of tape or aerosol overspray, and cleans up in a jiffy (1–1). As an economic measure, you can buy the cement in gallon containers, and then transfer it to smaller jars. And rather than peel off the pattern, you can remove it at your stationary belt sander, a technique that clearly flattens the workpiece's top surface.

There are times, however, when tracing a photocopied pattern directly onto the wood seems appropriate. When you do, be sure to use transfer paper (available at art-supply, craft-supply, and fabric stores), not carbon paper, because transfer paper won't stain the wood. Use white or yellow transfer paper for dark woods, and blue, red, or graphite for light ones.

1–1. *Many scrollsawyers use rubber cement for sticking on paper patterns because it's quick, holds the pattern firmly, and cleans up in a jiffy.*

USING PERMANENT PATTERNS

Paper patterns, of course, get cut up during the scrollsawing. Although it's easy enough to create another one at a copy machine, it's a better idea to make permanent templates for those patterns you'll frequently return to (**1–2**). You can use a variety of materials for templates, as long as the material is relatively tough and rigid—cardboard, file-folder stock, ⅛" hardboard, stencil board, and even plastic.

Another material that is good to use is plastic laminate, such as that used on countertops, because it's thin and durable. The advantages of using plastic templates are that you can fit many into a small box, they are inexpensive, and they don't wear out. It is recommended that you number the templates on the back and keep them referenced in a notebook, along with comments regarding each one's use. The easiest way to make plastic templates is to cut them out when you saw the project's basic shape, adhering the template material to the bottom of the workpiece with double-faced tape.

SCROLLSAWING MATERIALS

Wood has been the material of choice for scrollsawyers since the craft's birth. But all wood isn't equal, and that's due to density. Uniform density should be the first characteristic a scrollsawyer looks for when selecting stock, either hardwood or softwood. Why? Sawing across constantly changing densities makes for labored sawing. Softness allows the blade to spurt ahead. Encountering harder spots brings the blade almost to a halt. Steering wood that is of varying densities becomes a fight between soft areas grabbing the blade and harder ones deflecting it. Staying on the pattern line is difficult at best.

With both hardwood and softwood, you'll have better scrollsawing success with flat-sawn stock (stock with the end grain running parallel to the cutting surface). The vertical end grain of quartersawn stock tends to trap the blade in the soft part of a growth ring. This makes cutting along the stock's length difficult.

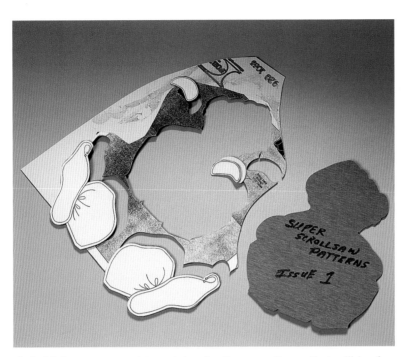

1–2. Make permanent templates for those patterns that will be frequently used. A variety of materials, including cardboard, ⅛" hardboard, and even plastic, can be used for templates.

Hardwoods and Softwoods

Among the hardwoods, you'll discover that basswood, butternut, cherry, oak, soft maple, walnut, and yellow poplar are agreeable stock for scrollsawing. In the softwoods, pine (**1–3**), cedar, and fir—especially dimensional construction stock—prove popular. All softwoods, though, don't always meet the uniform-density criteria, due to the usual difference between the hard, dark part of a growth ring and the soft, lighter-colored segment.

Looking for softwood stock that has less distinct rings is time well spent. You can also find economy in the lesser grades of hardwood and softwood, if you're willing to move your patterns around to diminish the effects of knots and other flaws. Lower grades may also adapt well to scrollsawn projects that you're going to paint anyway.

Remember, though, that solid stock—particularly thin material—tends to break where the grain runs across a narrow part of a pattern. If you can't adjust a pattern on the stock to avoid these potential breaks, you'll be better off using plywood.

Plywoods

Plywoods are the frequent choice for scrollsawing. Traditional softwood plywood is available in ⅟₁₆", ³⁄₁₆", ½", and ¾" thicknesses. Baltic-birch plywood and similar craft plywoods provide better stability, strength, and uniform density because of a greater number of plies. However, many of this type are sold in metric thicknesses for which you have to account in planning. The greatest advantage of these multilayer plywoods is their lack of interior voids. Hardwood plywood with a solid core presents another voidless option, and it's sold in thicknesses down to ¼" .

Metals

You might want to try non-ferrous metals, if they're soft. Aluminum and brass are the choices for scrollsawing—never try to saw ferrous metals, such iron and steel. Even if your scrollsaw is a single-speed model, you'll be able to handle light-duty metal cutting. With a two-speed or

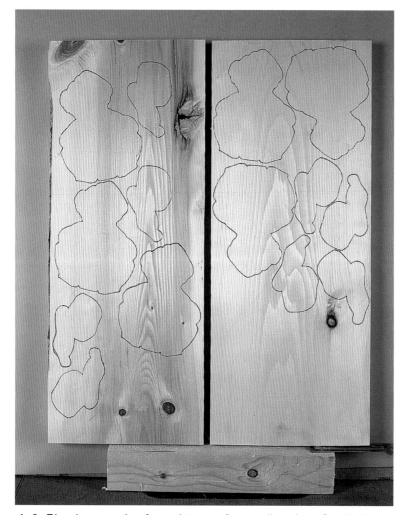

1–3. Pine is a good softwood to use for scrollsawing. On the left is No. 3 pine. On the right is No. 2 pine. No. 3 pine is less expensive, but has more knots. However, you can work around these defects to utilize most of the board.

stores, as well as many tool dealers, sell metal-piercing blades that fit ordinary scroll-saws (plain-end type blades). Remember, when you buy blades, buy plenty, because you'll break a lot of them as you get the hang of sawing metal.

A scrollsaw isn't as forgiving with metal as it is with wood. Some side pressure on the blade is possible when you saw wood, but in metal, it makes the blade heat up quickly, and then break. When cutting metal, always feed it directly into the blade at a moderate rate, and keep the force on the front of the blade when you go into curves and turns. Lubricating the blade helps, too. Beeswax is your best bet, but silicone spray, sewing-machine oil, petroleum jelly, and even kitchen shortening will work. Frequently reapply whatever you use to extend blade life.

To more easily scrollsaw thin sheet metal, put it between two pieces of ⅜" or ½" thick scrap wood. Secure it with tape, and then affix the pattern to the top of the wood.

For thicker metal, adhere the pattern to the top of the material with rubber cement

variable-speed machine, move down to a lower speed.

You won't even be able to cut soft metals, however, with blades designed for wood. Blades designed for soft-metal cutting are often called jeweler's metal-piercing blades. They're harder than traditional wood blades and have finer teeth. Although both wood-cutting blades and metal-piercing blades carry number designations, remember that a No. 6 scrollsaw blade and a No. 6 metal-piercing blade aren't the same! Mail-order woodworking suppliers and similar and cover the bottom of it with masking or other tape to avoid scratches. Be sure that you leave plenty of metal around the pattern to hang on to.

Know what to buy when you shop for metal. Aluminum up to ⅛" thick will scrollsaw well; any thicker takes patience and practice. You'll find suitable aluminum at home centers and some lumberyards, as well as at hobby shops and retail metal dealers. Avoid aluminum alloys unless you're familiar with them—some are much harder than normal aluminum.

Sheet brass is more difficult to come by. Hobby shops catering to model airplane and railroad enthusiasts are a good source. They often sell precut sheet brass of 1⁄16" or less thickness. For thicker material, you'll have to shop brass and copper dealers (try the Yellow Pages). But just like aluminum, ⅛" cuts best and ¼" is about the limit for scrollsawing. When you shop, ask for "half-hard" brass. Marine brass and bronze are too hard for scrollsaw cutting.

Aluminum and brass projects offer a variety of finishing techniques. First, though, you'll have to sand off any burrs around the edges. And

if your pattern calls for drilled holes, do them before finishing.

For a simple polishing, turn to polishing compound (tripoli works great) and a muslin buffing wheel mounted in your drill press or bench grinder. Wear gloves and eye protection when polishing because the wheel can catch the metal and send it flying. Note that polishing only requires minimal pressure against the wheel—the compound does the work.

If you want a brushed look, sand the metal with 400-, 600-, or 1200-grit abrasive. The coarser the grit, the rougher the finish. For a satin finish, apply automotive rubbing compound with a soft cloth. When you've achieved the desired look, protect the metal with several light coats of spray lacquer, letting each coat dry before adding another.

Many plastics adapt to scrollsawing, too. There's a catch, however. Some plastics (called thermoplastics) readily melt or deform when heated. This means that the scrollsaw blade generates enough heat to make the kerf close behind it and fuse. Using a low speed helps this problem. So does installing a wider, thicker blade with coarser teeth. With plastics, it's always smart to

test cut a small sample before purchasing enough for a whole project.

CHOOSING SCROLLSAW BLADES

Know Your Blade Options

There's no lack of choices when you shop for scrollsaw blades. Here are some points to keep in mind when you buy:

• *Choose plain-end blades instead of pin-end.* Most scrollsaws nowadays accept plain-end blades, utilizing built-in blade clamps or separate blade-end fixtures. Attaching separate clamps (required by some saws) takes extra time, but the plain-end blade's advantages outweigh the inconvenience.

Plain-end blades can cut inside a tiny pattern area because they'll slip through a 1⁄16" hole, or even smaller. Pin-ends require a 9⁄64" start hole. You'll also spend less for plain-end blades, and have a greater selection in size and tooth style. Pin-end blades are easier to install, but they're thicker and wider than the largest plain-end blades. They are good candidates for simple patterns in thick stock, if your saw will take them. If so, you should choose 5" plain-end blades.

• *Remember, blade teeth do the cutting.* Scrollsaw blades come in five traditional tooth patterns. You need to be familiar with them and what each can do best.

• **Standard pattern blades.** These blades, sometimes called skip-tooth or fretsaw blades, feature wide gullets between teeth that quickly clear chips and aid cooling. These fast, smooth-cutting blades can handle nearly all your scrollsawing needs. That's why they're best sellers.

• **Double-tooth blades.** These blades also have wide gullets to clear chips, but will put more teeth into thin stock for smoother cuts. They're only available with plain ends.

• **Scrollsaw blades.** These blades were pretty much standard equipment on the old rigid-arm jigsaws. Thicker, wider, and coarser than the skip-tooth blades, they lend themselves best to straight cutting or cutting simple curves in heavy stock.

• **Reverse-tooth blades.** These blades look like standard blades except for the half dozen or so teeth at the bottom pointing the other way. They do what they were designed to do: reduce tearout and chipping on the bottom of the workpiece. But, they also reduce cutting speed. However, for thin stock and plywood prone to tearout, they work well.

• **Spiral blades.** These blades have a twist to them which permits cutting from all directions. Theoretically, you wouldn't have to turn the workpiece with one of these in your scrollsaw. Although they cut a wide, not-so-smooth kerf, they're the only blade that can cut bevels in the same direction on opposite edges of a workpiece.

How to Select the Right Blade

Few professional scroll-sawyers maintain a complete selection of all the blades available. Most settle on just the few that they've found work well for them. With a bit of experimentation, you'll find which blades work the best for you. But if you remember only one thing when selecting a blade, let it be this rule: Get the coarsest (fewest teeth per inch), widest blade that will give you a satisfactorily smooth cut for the job at hand (**1–4**). Here's why:

Blade width, measured from the front of the teeth to the back edge, determines a blade's maneuverability. Narrow blades (with lower number designations) can make sharper turns than wide blades. On the other hand, narrow blades won't track as well on straight cuts because they tend to wander. So, choosing which blade to use depends a lot on the type(s) of patterns you like or plan to do.

Use this approach in your experimentation: Try coarser blades first. Coarser blades cut faster and may last a bit longer than finer-toothed ones, but the cut may not be as smooth as you like. On the other hand, fine-toothed blades produce smoother cuts, but cut more slowly, thus creating excessive heat that may result in burnt edges. What you want to work toward is a livable compromise between speed and smoothness of cut.

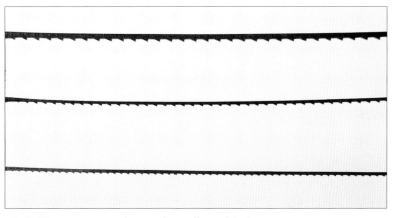

1–4. Three commonly used scrollsaw blades.

Blades the Pros Choose

Iowa scroller Rick Hutcheson relies on only three sizes of skip-tooth blades for nearly all of his work. He uses a No. 5 blade for ¾" pine, oak, walnut, and most other woods, and a No. 2 blade for thin Baltic-birch plywoods (⅛", ³⁄₁₆", or ½"). He cuts a stack of these about ¾" thick and gets good detail with a minimum of feathering on the bottom. For the extra strength needed in sawing woods more than 1" thick, he uses a relatively thick and wide No. 9 blade. It's possible to run this blade at 2,000 rpm in 1½" thick pine and fir without it heating up.

The Chicago-area scrollsawing team of Roy King and Scott Kochendorfer cut their intricate designs with a No. 2 blade because with that blade, you can spin the workpiece, make 90- and 45-degree cuts, and do other techniques easily.

Minnesota fretwork scroll-sawyer Carl Weckhorst likes to use reverse-tooth blades for smooth, splinter-free cuts on both sides of his workpieces. He uses a No. 2 blade for ⅛" stock. For ¼" to ½" stock, he uses a No. 5. For heavy ¾" stock, he uses a No. 20 blade with only about 9 teeth per inch.

TEN TIPS FOR SCROLLSAWING PLEASURE

1 **Square up your saw table easily.** To make tight turns and keep square edges on your workpieces, the saw table must be at a 90-degree angle to the blade. Ensure square cuts by making a ⅛" deep cut into the face of a 1½" thick piece of scrap-wood. Then, swing the wood around so that the cut faces you, and place the cut behind the blade (**1–5**). If the back of the blade doesn't fit into this kerf, adjust the table until it does.

2 **Keep plenty of blades at hand.** A blade may only last through 20 minutes of hard cutting before you have to change it. So trim the length of these interruptions by keeping blades within reach on magnetic strips. Fasten two 4"-long magnets (found at hobby and hardware stores) to scraps of ½" thick scrap wood. Fasten

1–5. Test the fit of the blade in the kerf to see if your scroll-saw's table is square.

1–6. Make this handy scrollsaw blade holder from magnetic strips and scrapwood.

the assemblies to your workbench near the scrollsaw base, about 3" apart (**1–6**). The holders keep the blades going in the same direction and sawdust-free.

3 Relax for concentration. Keep your body relaxed by sitting on a high stool when you scrollsaw. With your hands and forearms at saw-table height, you'll be better able to concentrate on the workpiece and you will not tire as easily.

4 Get back to the pattern line. Staying right on the pattern line isn't critical for most patterns. If you wander, just try to get smoothly back (as shown in **1–7**), rather than backing up and recutting. How far you can safely wander depends on the size of what you're cutting. No one would notice a ¼" error on a 12" flower, but the same size error on a 2" flower would be much more visible.

5 Remove fuzz in a jiffy. You can quickly remove the inevitable fuzz and feathering on the back side of a scrollsawn workpiece by placing it facedown on a piece of carpet pad, and then sanding the back with 120-grit abrasive in a finishing sander (**1–8**). The pad securely grips the wood.

6 Save your wood to the right. Because scrollsaw blades are stamped from thin sheet steel, there's always a burr to the right of their teeth. That is, as you look at the blade secured in the saw with the teeth pointing down, the burr is to your right. If you remember to always keep your "save" piece (the project) to the right of the blade when cutting, you'll have more control and you will be able to make tighter turns (**1–9**).

7 Turn to a cutting platform for thin stock. A cutting platform gives you near-blade support for cutting thin silhouettes (**1–10**). Make

1–7. If you stray from the pattern line, make a smooth recovery and no one will notice.

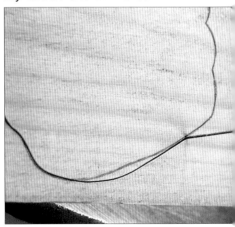

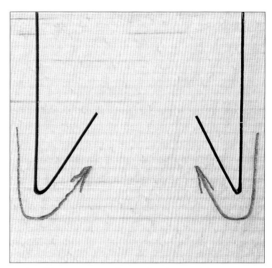

1–9. Keep your "save" piece (the project piece) on the right side of the blade. This allows more control over the cut and tighter turns. This photo shows the same cut made with the save piece to the right and left of the blade, as shown by the arrows. With the save piece to the left, the scrollsawyer had to take a wider turn, and removed more material at the turning point.

1–8. To quickly remove fuzz and feathering on the back side of a scrollsawn workpiece, place it facedown on a piece of carpet pad, and then sand the back with 120-grit abrasive in a finishing sander.

one the same size as your saw table from smooth wood and drill a "zero-clearance" 1/8" hole (for a No. 2 blade) in its center. Clamp down the auxiliary table or fasten it with double-faced tape. Such a table can also extend the useful life of your blades if you install it when a blade starts

1–10. To support a thin blade, make a cutting platform with a zero-clearance blade hole.

1–11. Unlike drill bits, brads won't break out the wood on the workpiece's backside when drilling blade start holes.

several pieces of wood together in a stack for multiple cutting. But nails and screws can sometimes split the wood or stick through the stack to mar the saw table. Removing double-faced tape is time consuming, and pieces can break off. You can hold a stack of pieces together with dowels cut just shorter than the depth of the stack. Simply drill appropriately sized holes in waste areas of the stack and insert the dowels.

to dull, because it raises the workpiece to the upper teeth, which normally receive little wear.

8 **You'll have no break out with brads.** Use a brad of the appropriate size (to fit your blade) chucked into a drill to drill the inside blade start holes of a pattern (**1–11**). Brads leave clean exit holes compared to drill bits.

9 **Keep your eyes slightly ahead of the blade when cutting a curve.** You'll have

greater success if you focus your eyes on a point about 1/16" in front of the blade when cutting a curve.

10 **Ease up on pressure.** The less pressure you put on the workpiece, the more control you'll have. Try to relax your arm and chest muscles when cutting, and let your fingertips do the work.

11 **Stick stacks together with dowels.** Nails, screws, and double-faced tape are commonly used to fasten

TABLE 1 –1.	Blades at a Glance			
(Standard, skip-tooth, and plain-end blades listed)				
UNIVERSAL NUMBER	WIDTH (INCH)	THICKNESS (INCH)	TEETH PER INCH	APPLICATIONS
2/0	.015–.022	.010	28–30	Extemely intricate sawing in veneers, plastics, hard rubber, and pearl up to ³⁄₃₂" thick
0	.024	.011	25	
1	.026	.011–.012	23–25	
2	.028–.029	.012–.013	20–23	Tight radius, work in hardwoods to ½" thick, softwoods to ¾", and plastics to ¼"
3	.032	.013–.014	18–20	
4	.035	.014–.015	15–18	
5	.038–.039	.015–.016	12½–16½	Tight radius, work in hardwoods up to ¾" thick, softwoods to 1", and plastics to ½"
6	.041–.043	.016–.017	12½–15	
7	.045	.017–.018	11½–14	Hardwoods to 1", softwoods to 1½", plastics to ½"
8	.047–.049	.017–.018	11½–14	
9	.053	.018–.019	11½–14	
10	.056–.057	.019–.020	11–12½	Hardwoods to 1½", softwoods to 2", plastics to ⅝"
11	.059–.063	.019–.020	9½–12½	
12	.062	.024	9½	

KEEPING YOUR SCROLLSAWING ACCIDENT-FREE

Scrollsawing is a thoroughly enjoyable woodworking experience. But we all know that accidents can happen. Reduce their possibility by following this advice:

● Get to know your scrollsaw. Read the owner's manual and follow it to properly set up, adjust, and maintain your saw.

● Plug your scrollsaw into a properly grounded outlet. If you must use an extension cord, make sure it is heavy enough—at least 14-gauge—and in safe condition.

● Always be sure that the blade is properly tensioned before you start the saw. Check also that its teeth are pointing down and that all table-tilt knobs are adjusted and tightened.

● Keep sawdust out of your way. Set the machine's sawdust blower to direct airflow away from you, preferably toward the back of the saw.

● Wear eye protection. Goggles or shielded safety glasses keep flying debris from the saw or the wood out of your eyes.

● Dress with common sense. Don't wear loose-fitting clothing or dangling jewelry. Tie back long hair or wear a cap.

● Control the workpiece. Adjust the hold-down as necessary.

Keep the workpiece flat on the table and never cut when it is unsupported. If the work catches on the blade, turn off the saw. A foot-operated on/off switch will prove helpful, because boths hands are free to control the workpiece (**1–12**).

● Keep your work area tidy. Never let sawdust and cut-off pieces accumulate around the saw. Allow for task lighting that lets you clearly see the blade.

1–12. A foot-operated on/off switch will prove to be a helpful accessory because it allows the operator to use both hands to control the workpiece.

FUN-FILLED PATTERNS FOR THE BEGINNER

2

Quick-and-Easy Cuts

If you're new to the scrollsaw and unfamiliar with all its capabilities, the patterns in this chapter are just right for you. Although not complicated, and intended for thin stock (3/8"-thick or less), they offer you the opportunity to learn control by taking you through gentle curves and sharply formed edges. Their simple designs also lend themselves to multiple cutting (refer to Chapter 1, page 18) so that you can make several of each for family and friends.

Tabletop Reindeer

Tabletop reindeer.

EXPLODED AND ASSEMBLY VIEWS

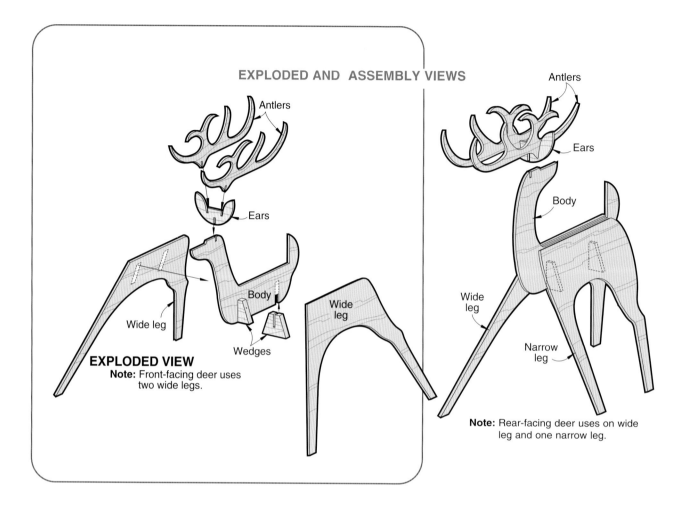

Antlers

Ears

Wide leg

Body

Wedges

EXPLODED VIEW
Note: Front-facing deer uses
two wide legs.

Wide
leg

Antlers

Ears

Body

Wide
leg

Narrow
leg

Note: Rear-facing deer uses on wide
leg and one narrow leg.

MATERIALS LIST...

- *⅛"-thick birch plywood*
- *strip of ⅜ × 1½ × 12" plywood*
- *paint*

NOTE: *The patterns for this project
are shown at full size (100%).*

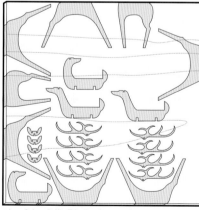

⅛ x 24 x 24" Birch plywood

⅜ x 1½ x 12" Plywood

*Cutting diagram
for the tabletop
reindeer. This
diagram is for
two rear-facing
deer, and two
front-facing deer.*

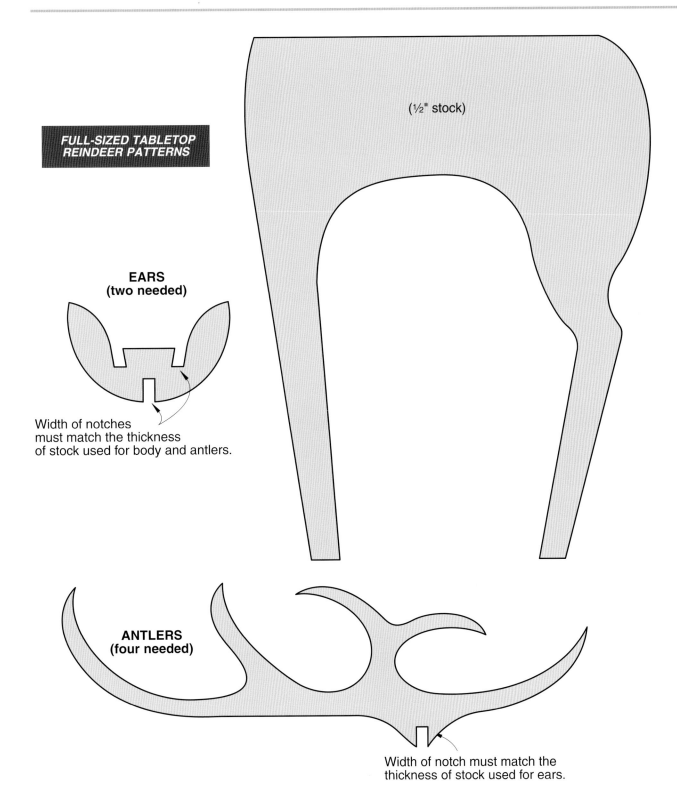

FULL-SIZED TABLETOP REINDEER PATTERNS

(½" stock)

EARS
(two needed)

Width of notches
must match the thickness
of stock used for body and antlers.

ANTLERS
(four needed)

Width of notch must match the
thickness of stock used for ears.

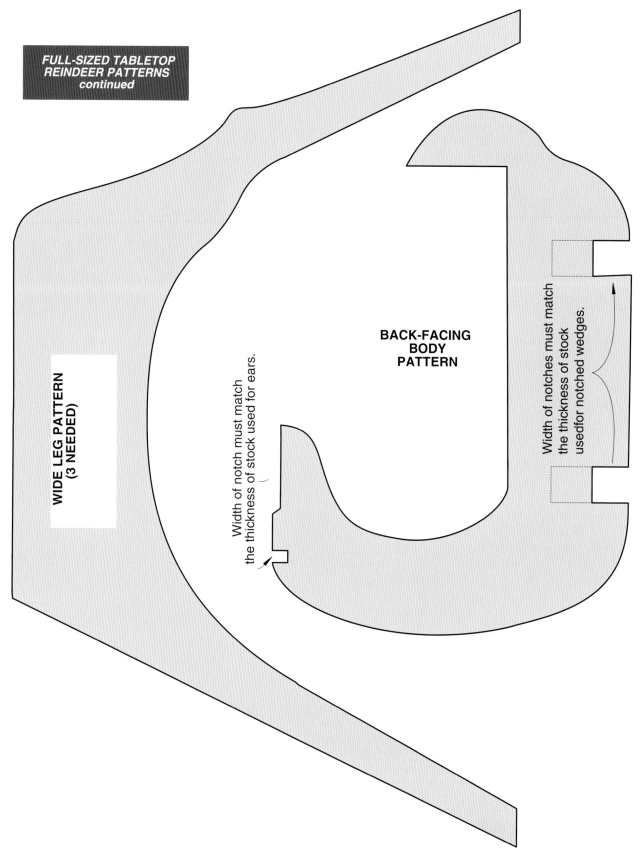

FULL-SIZED TABLETOP REINDEER PATTERNS
continued

WIDE LEG PATTERN (3 NEEDED)

BACK-FACING BODY PATTERN

Width of notch must match the thickness of stock used for ears.

Width of notches must match the thickness of stock used for notched wedges.

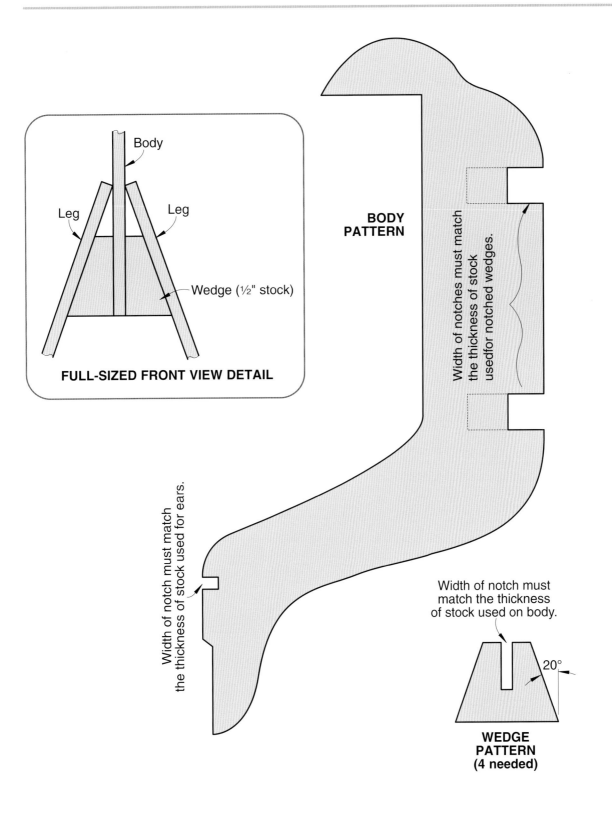

Body

Leg

Leg

Wedge (½" stock)

FULL-SIZED FRONT VIEW DETAIL

**BODY
PATTERN**

Width of notches must match
the thickness of stock
usedfor notched wedges.

Width of notch must match
the thickness of stock used for ears.

Width of notch must
match the thickness
of stock used on body.

20°

**WEDGE
PATTERN
(4 needed)**

Romping Reptiles

TYRANNASAURUS

TRICERATOPS

BRONTOSAURUS

MATERIALS LIST...✎

- ⅛"-thick birch plywood
- paint

NOTE: The patterns for this project are shown at full size (100%).

**TRICERATOPS
BACK LEGS PATTERN**

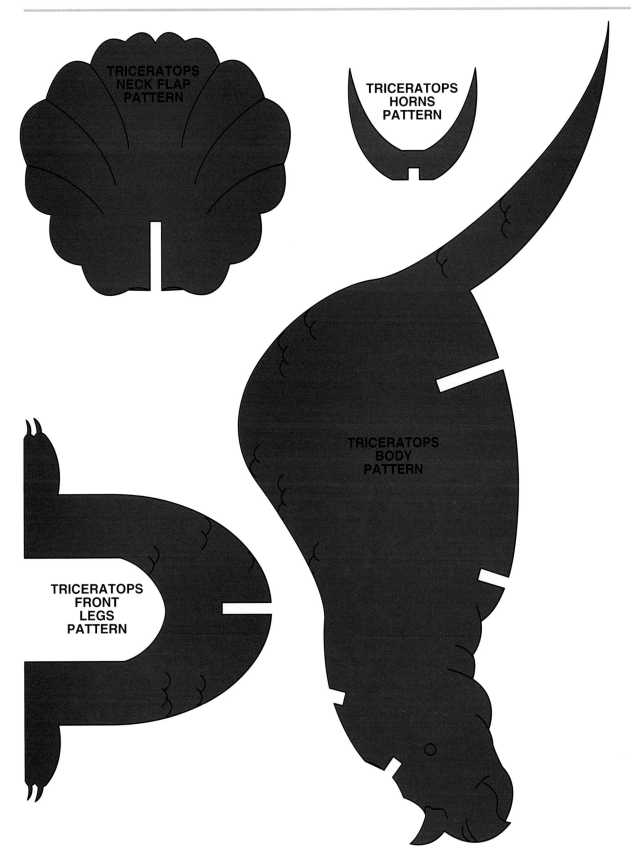

TRICERATOPS
NECK FLAP
PATTERN

TRICERATOPS
HORNS
PATTERN

TRICERATOPS
BODY
PATTERN

TRICERATOPS
FRONT
LEGS
PATTERN

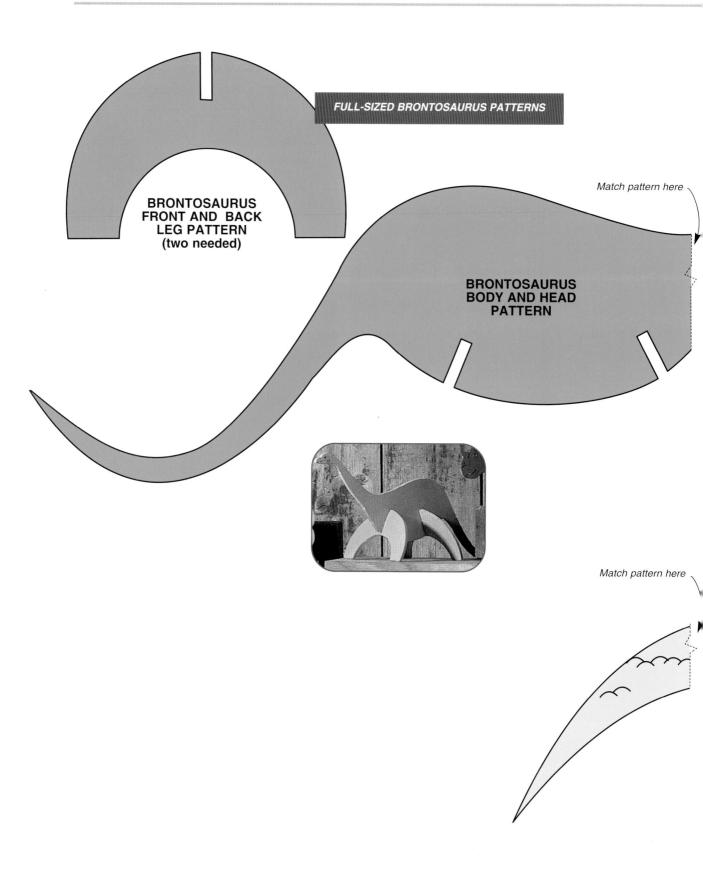

FULL-SIZED BRONTOSAURUS PATTERNS

**BRONTOSAURUS
FRONT AND BACK
LEG PATTERN**
(two needed)

Match pattern here

**BRONTOSAURUS
BODY AND HEAD
PATTERN**

Match pattern here

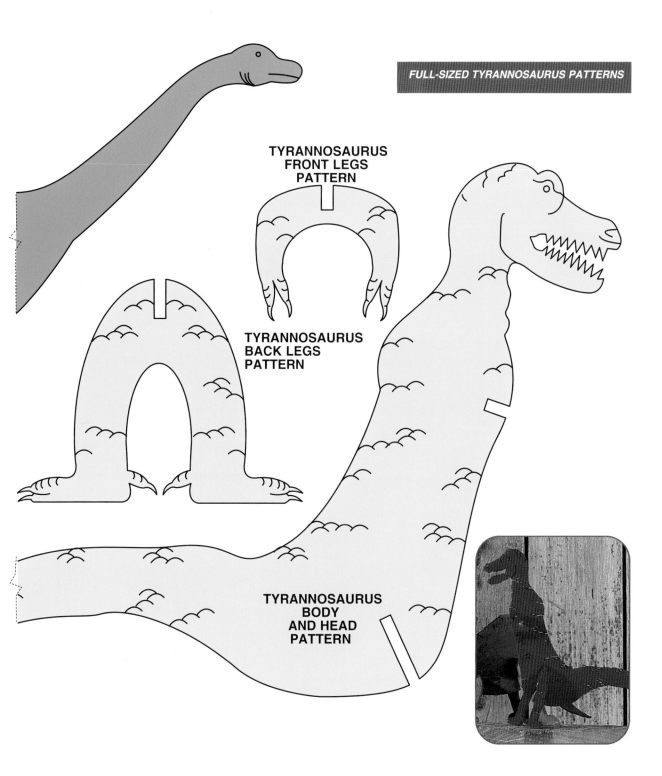

FULL-SIZED TYRANNOSAURUS PATTERNS

**TYRANNOSAURUS
FRONT LEGS
PATTERN**

**TYRANNOSAURUS
BACK LEGS
PATTERN**

**TYRANNOSAURUS
BODY
AND HEAD
PATTERN**

Dangling Dinosaurs

MATERIALS LIST...

- $\frac{1}{8}$"-thick birch plywood or posterboard
- acrylic paints, water colors, or a clear finish
- fishing line or heavy thread

NOTE: The patterns for this project are shown at full size (100%).

PTERANODON

PTERODACTYL

PTERODACTYL

TYRANNOSAURUS

BRONTOSAUR

TRICERATOPS

STEGOSAURUS

FULL-SIZED DANGLING DINOSAURS PATTERNS

$1/16$" hole

$1/16$" hole

**TRICERATOPS
PATTERN**

**TYRANNOSAURUS
PATTERN**

PTERODACTYL PATTERN
(two needed)

PTERODACTYL WING PATTERN
(two needed)

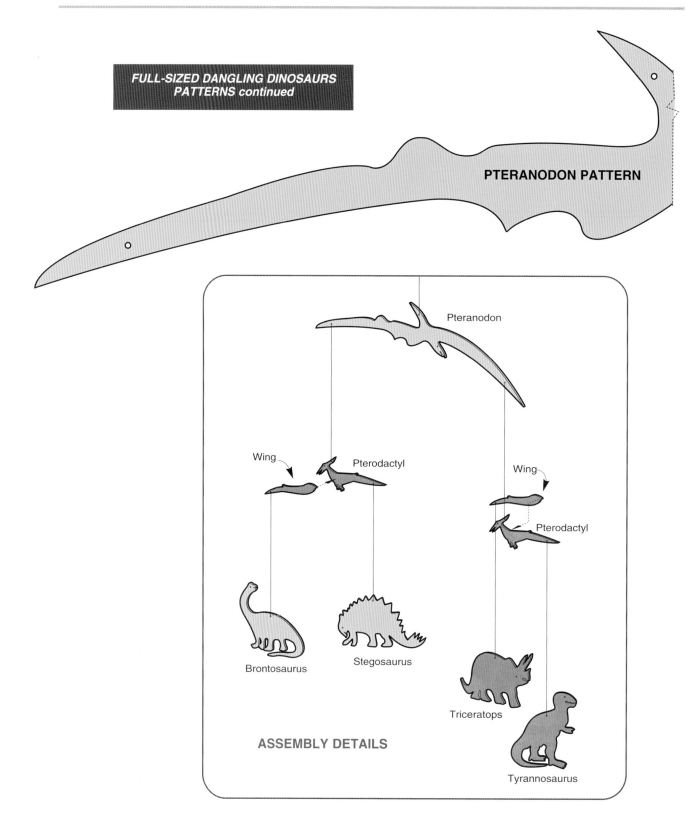

FULL-SIZED DANGLING DINOSAURS PATTERNS continued

PTERANODON PATTERN

Pteranodon

Wing

Pterodactyl

Wing

Pterodactyl

Brontosaurus

Stegosaurus

Triceratops

Tyrannosaurus

ASSEMBLY DETAILS

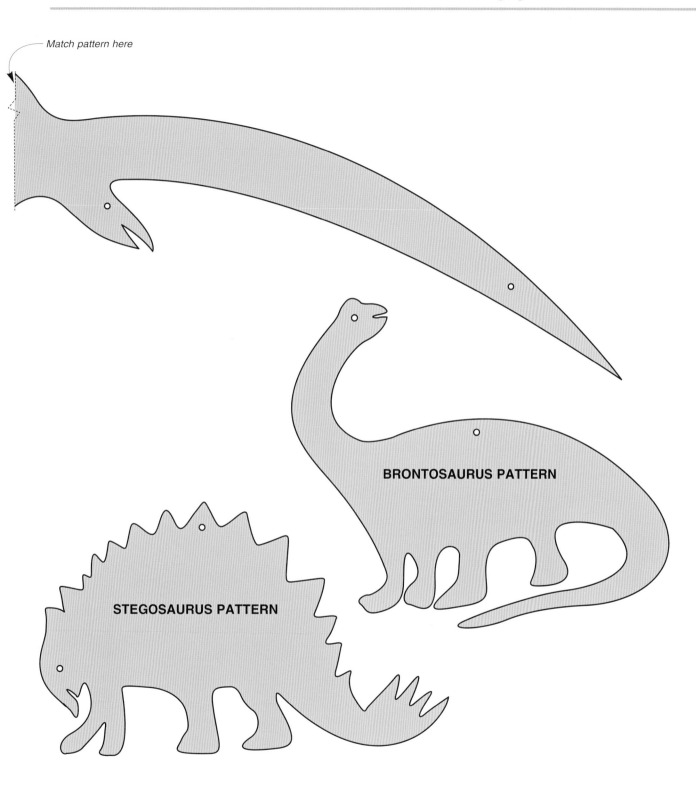

Match pattern here

BRONTOSAURUS PATTERN

STEGOSAURUS PATTERN

Cedar Closet Hangers

MATERIALS LIST...

- ⅜"-thick aromatic cedar
- paint
- fishing line
- heavy thread

NOTE: The patterns for this project are shown at full size (100%).

CATS PATTERN

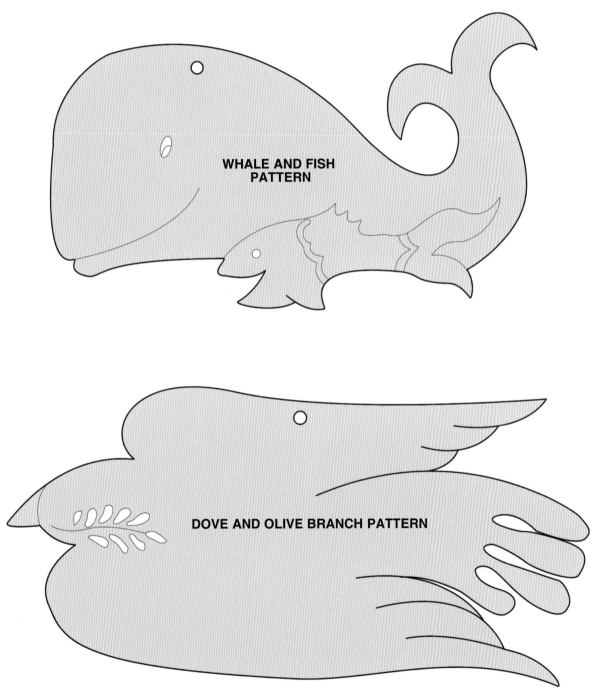

WHALE AND FISH PATTERN

DOVE AND OLIVE BRANCH PATTERN

Tree Trimmers

SAWING THE PARTS TO SHAPE

1 Make copies of the full-sized ornaments. The patterns for each ornament's body and onlay are combined, so you'll need two copies for each ornament you wish to make.

2 Prepare your stock. Each ornament consists of one ⅛"-thick body and two ¹⁄₁₆"-thick onlays, as shown in the Exploded View drawing. Resaw and plane the ⅛" stock, and resaw and drum-sand the ¹⁄₁₆" stock. You'll need one ⅛ × 3½ × 6" and two ¹⁄₁₆ × 3½ × 6" pieces of stock for each ornament you wish to make. (Maple and cherry are good choices.) Adhere the patterns to the stock, arranging the patterns so that each part's longest dimension is parallel to the wood grain. To save copies and time, stack-cut the parts, taping together two pieces of ¹⁄₁₆" onlay stock for each piece of ⅛" body stock.

3 Scrollsaw the parts to the pattern lines. A No. 2 blade with 20 teeth per inch works nicely. To make a zero-clearance table insert for scrollsawing the tiny parts, cover the insert with a couple of layers of 2"-wide plastic packaging tape. The shaded areas on the angel and dove

MATERIALS LIST...

- ⅛" and ¹⁄₁₆"-thick hardwood stock (maple and cherry used here) or ⅛"-thick birch plywood
- Glue
- Paint
- 18-gauge copper wire to hang

NOTE: The patterns for this project are shown at full size (100%).

patterns designate cutouts in the bodies. Drill blade start holes in these areas, and saw them out. Drill the ⅛" holes in the tree onlays with a brad-point bit.

4 Remove the patterns. If they don't peel off easily, blot them with lacquer thinner. Remove adhesive residue from the wood by wiping it with a clean rag and more thinner. Smooth any rough edges with 220-grit sandpaper.

ASSEMBLING AND FINISHING THE TREE TRIMMERS

1 Before gluing the tree onlays to the tree body, position one onlay on each side, tracing lightly around it with a pencil. Set the onlay aside, and paint the body with acrylic craft paint, staying inside the marked lines, as shown at top right.

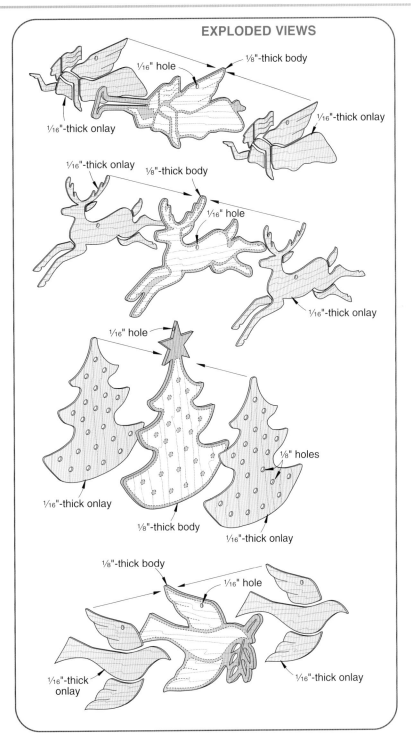

EXPLODED VIEWS

1/16" hole

⅛"-thick body

1/16"-thick onlay

1/16"-thick onlay

1/16"-thick onlay

⅛"-thick body

1/16" hole

1/16"-thick onlay

1/16" hole

⅛" holes

1/16"-thick onlay

⅛"-thick body

1/16"-thick onlay

⅛"-thick body

1/16" hole

1/16"-thick onlay

1/16"-thick onlay

Paint the portion of the tree body covered by the onlay. Stay about 1/16" back from the traced pencil lines. Erase the lines after the paint dries.

2 Glue the onlays to the bodies, positioning them as shown in the pattern.

3 Drill ¹⁄₁₆" holes through the ornaments for the decorative hooks, as shown on the patterns.

4 Sand the ornaments to 320 grit. Apply a clear finish. We used three coats of aerosol satin lacquer.

5 To make decorative ornament hangers, cut one 9"-long piece of 18-gauge copper wire for each ornament. Then make the ornament hangers, slip the completed hangers through the holes, and hang the ornaments. Twist the hooks for the best display angle.

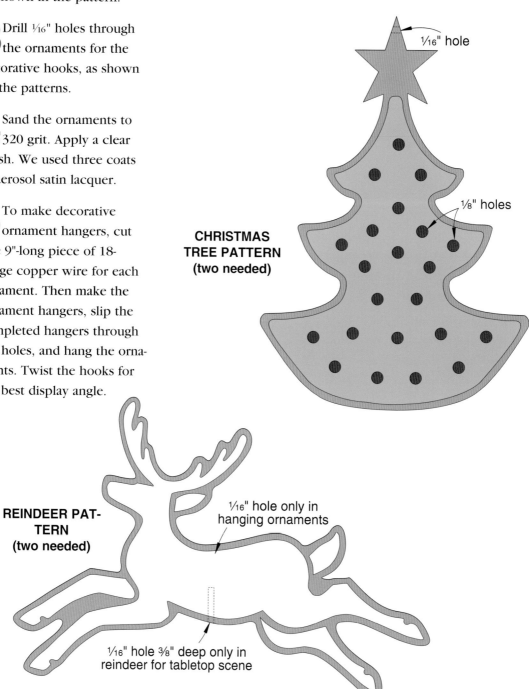

FULL-SIZED TREE TRIMMERS PATTERNS

¹⁄₁₆" hole

¹⁄₈" holes

CHRISTMAS TREE PATTERN (two needed)

REINDEER PATTERN (two needed)

¹⁄₁₆" hole only in hanging ornaments

¹⁄₁₆" hole ³⁄₈" deep only in reindeer for tabletop scene

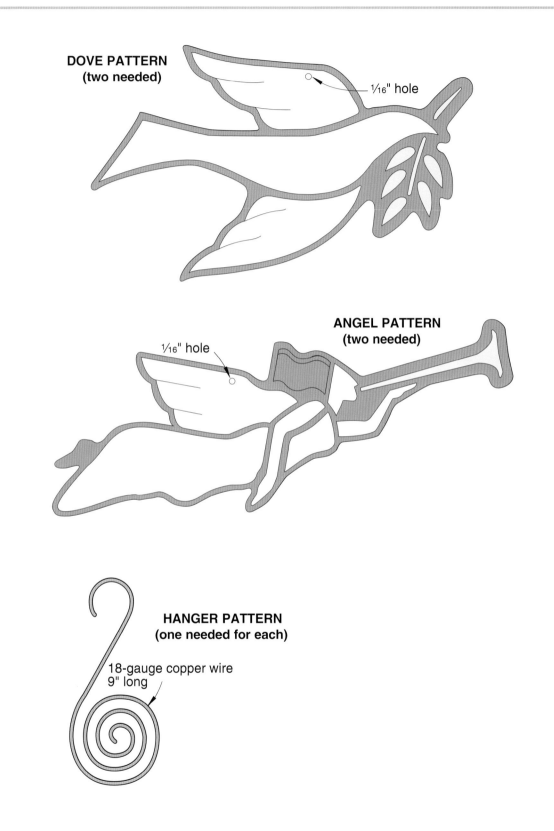

DOVE PATTERN
(two needed)

¹⁄₁₆" hole

ANGEL PATTERN
(two needed)

¹⁄₁₆" hole

HANGER PATTERN
(one needed for each)

18-gauge copper wire
9" long

3

Working with Thicker Stock

In the previous chapter, you fed thin stock through your scrollsaw, which was probably fitted with a lower-numbered blade (No. 4 or less). But many of the projects in this chapter are meant to be made from much thicker stock (3/4" to 1 1/2"). For those projects, you should switch to a higher-numbered blade, such as a No. 7, 8, or 9.

Kid's First Car

MATERIALS LIST... ✏

- 1½" thick stock (for body)
- ¾"-thick stock (for wheels)
- ¼"-diameter dowels
- Glue
- Paint

NOTE: The patterns for this project are shown at full size (100%).

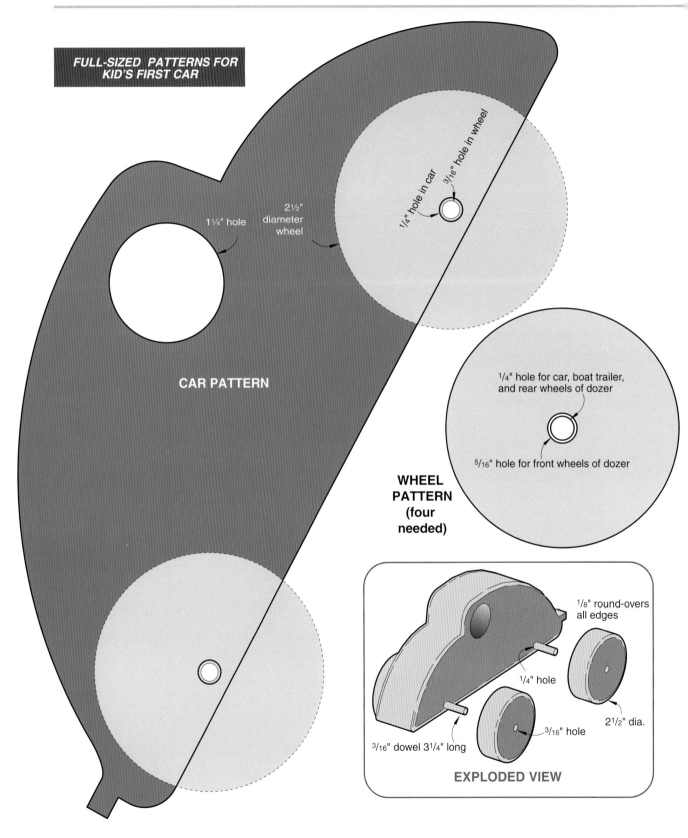

FULL-SIZED PATTERNS FOR KID'S FIRST CAR

1¼" hole

2½" diameter wheel

¼" hole in car

3/16" hole in wheel

CAR PATTERN

¼" hole for car, boat trailer, and rear wheels of dozer

5/16" hole for front wheels of dozer

WHEEL PATTERN (four needed)

⅛" round-overs all edges

¼" hole

2½" dia.

3/16" hole

3/16" dowel 3¼" long

EXPLODED VIEW

Land and Sea Combo

MATERIALS LIST...

- *1½"-thick stock (for body)*
- *¾"-thick stock (for wheels)*
- *⅜" diameter dowels*
- *Glue*
- *Paint*

NOTE: *The patterns for this project are shown at full size (100%).*

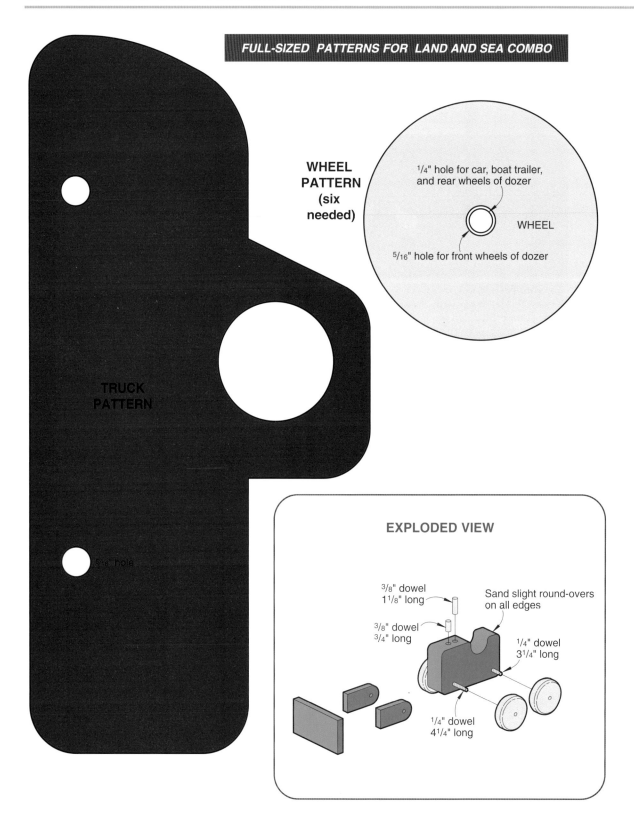

FULL-SIZED PATTERNS FOR LAND AND SEA COMBO

WHEEL PATTERN (six needed)

1/4" hole for car, boat trailer, and rear wheels of dozer

WHEEL

5/16" hole for front wheels of dozer

TRUCK PATTERN

5/16" hole

EXPLODED VIEW

3/8" dowel 1 1/8" long

3/8" dowel 3/4" long

Sand slight round-overs on all edges

1/4" dowel 3 1/4" long

1/4" dowel 4 1/4" long

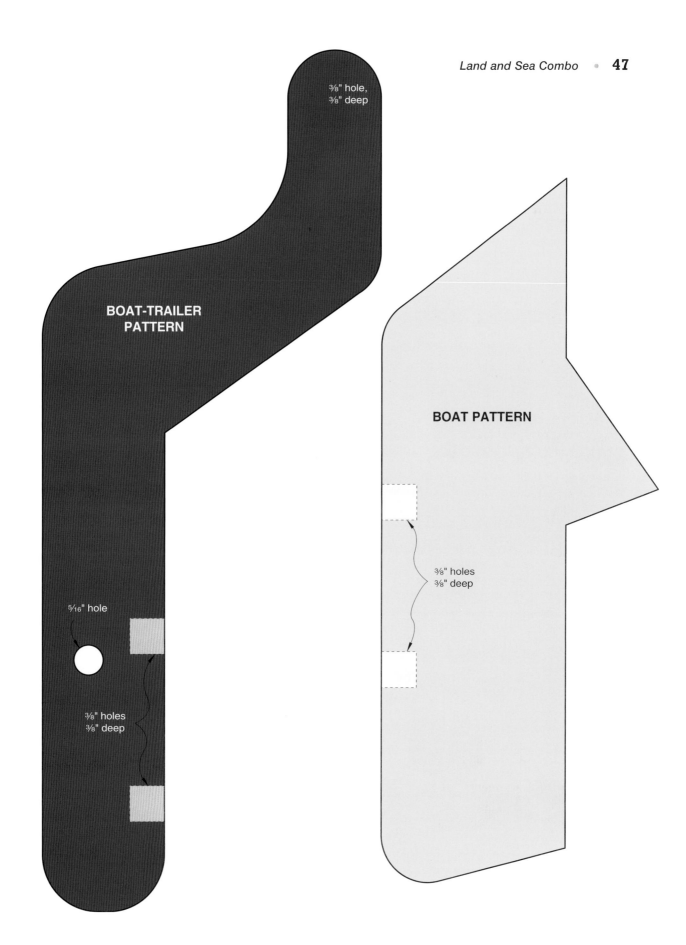

⅜" hole,
⅜" deep

**BOAT-TRAILER
PATTERN**

BOAT PATTERN

⅜" holes
⅜" deep

⁵⁄₁₆" hole

⅜" holes
⅜" deep

Little Buddy Bulldozer

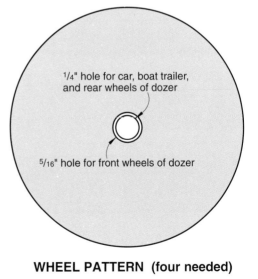

MATERIALS LIST...

- 1½"-thick stock (for body)
- ¾"-thick stock (for wheels)
- ½"-thick stock (for blade)
- ⅜"- and ¼"-diameter dowels
- Glue
- Paint

NOTE: The patterns for this project are shown at full size (100%).

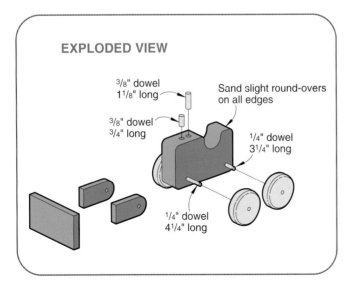

EXPLODED VIEW

³/₈" dowel 1¹/₈" long

³/₈" dowel ¾" long

Sand slight round-overs on all edges

¼" dowel 3¹/₄" long

¼" dowel 4¹/₄" long

¼" hole for car, boat trailer, and rear wheels of dozer

⁵/₁₆" hole for front wheels of dozer

WHEEL PATTERN (four needed)

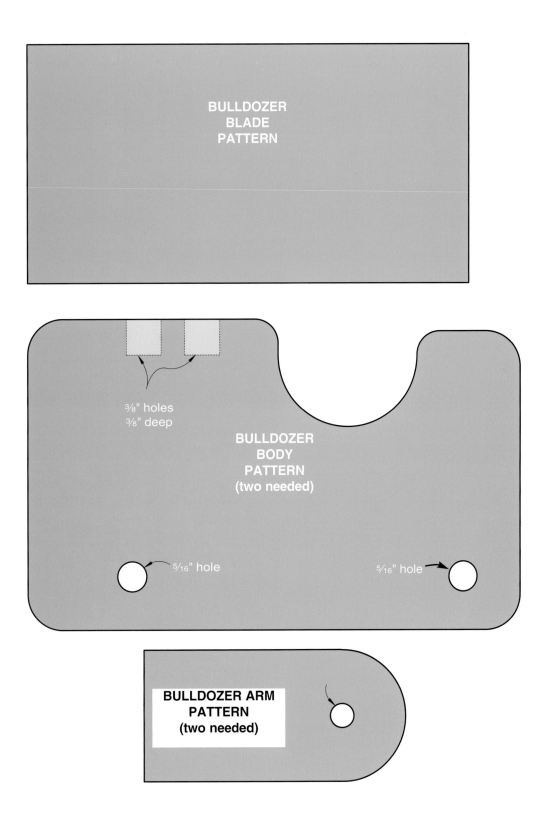

BULLDOZER
BLADE
PATTERN

⅜" holes
⅜" deep

BULLDOZER
BODY
PATTERN
(two needed)

⁵⁄₁₆" hole   ⁵⁄₁₆" hole

**BULLDOZER ARM
PATTERN
(two needed)**

Over-the-Rug Hauler

MATERIALS LIST... ✏

- 1½"-thick stock (for body)
- ⅜"-thick stock (for wheels)
- ¼"- and ⅜"-diameter dowels
- Glue
- Clear finish

NOTE: The patterns for this project are shown at 75%. For full-size, they must be enlarged to 133%

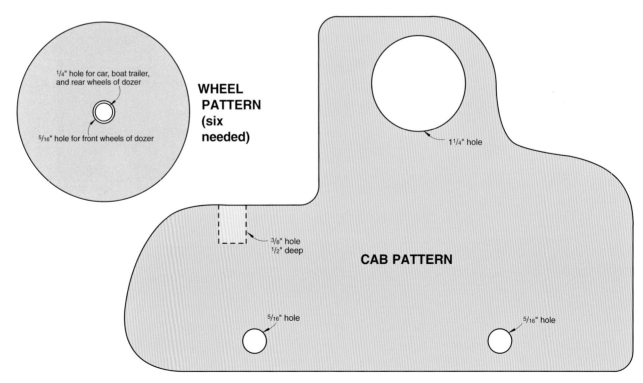

¼" hole for car, boat trailer, and rear wheels of dozer

⁵⁄₁₆" hole for front wheels of dozer

WHEEL PATTERN (six needed)

1¼" hole

⅜" hole ½" deep

CAB PATTERN

⁵⁄₁₆" hole

⁵⁄₁₆" hole

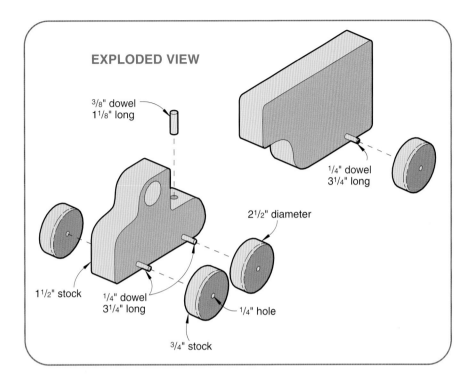

EXPLODED VIEW

$3/8$" dowel
$1 1/8$" long

$1/4$" dowel
$3 1/4$" long

$2 1/2$" diameter

$1 1/2$" stock

$1/4$" dowel
$3 1/4$" long

$1/4$" hole

$3/4$" stock

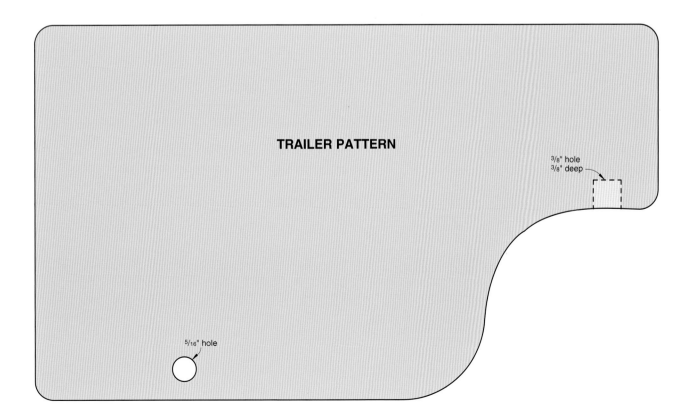

TRAILER PATTERN

$3/8$" hole
$3/8$" deep

$5/16$" hole

Big Top Circus

This three-ring circus has phenomenal patterns that include elephants, seals, poodles, high-wire artists, and a prancing pony.

MATERIALS LIST....

- ⅛"-thick birch plywood or posterboard
- ¾"-thick hardwood (for base)
- ¹⁄₁₆"-diameter dowels
- glue
- clear finish

NOTE: The patterns for this project are shown at full size (100%).

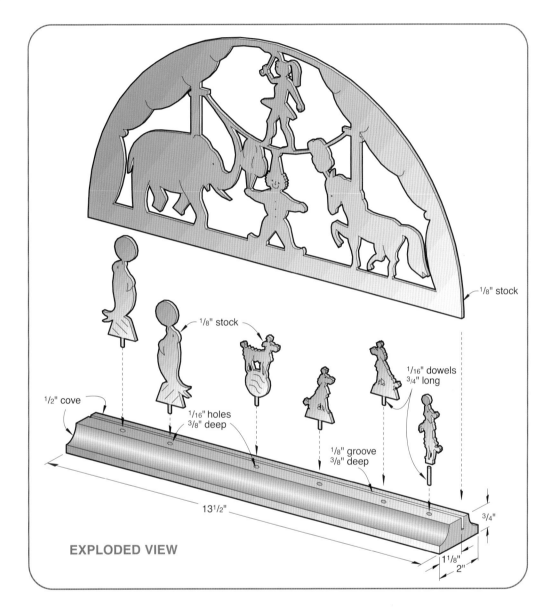

1/8" stock

1/8" stock

1/16" dowels
3/4" long

1/2" cove

1/16" holes
3/8" deep

1/8" groove
3/8" deep

3/4"

13 1/2"

1 1/8"

2"

EXPLODED VIEW

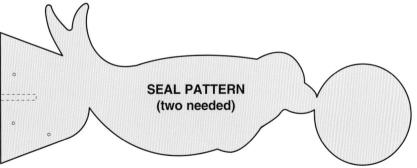

SEAL PATTERN
(two needed)

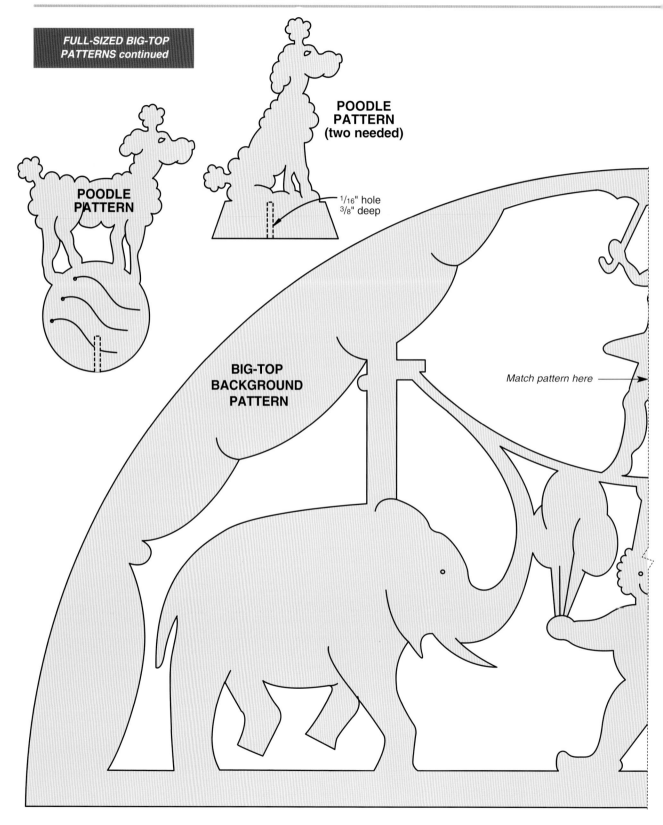

FULL-SIZED BIG-TOP PATTERNS continued

POODLE PATTERN (two needed)

POODLE PATTERN

1/16" hole
3/8" deep

BIG-TOP BACKGROUND PATTERN

Match pattern here

**POODLE
PATTERN**

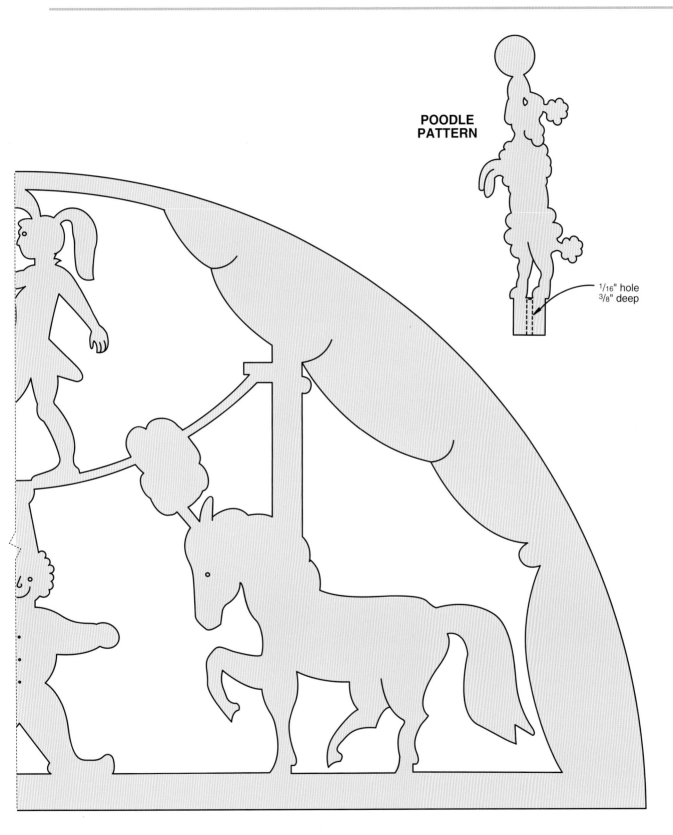

$^1/_{16}$" hole
$^3/_8$" deep

Desktop Dolphin

MATERIALS LIST...

- ¼"- and ¾"-thick maple (or other stock)
- ¼"- and ½"-thick walnut (or other stock)
- Glue
- Clear finish

NOTE: The patterns for this project are shown at full size (100%).

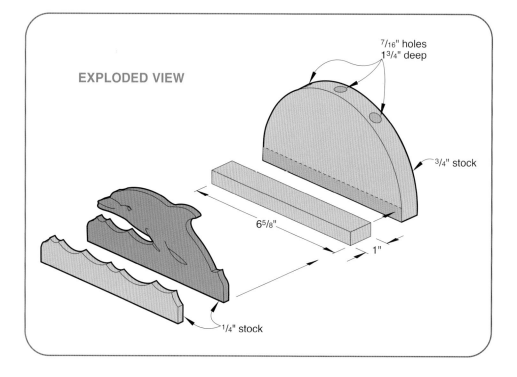

EXPLODED VIEW

7/16" holes
1³/₄" deep

3/4" stock

6⁵/₈"

1"

1/4" stock

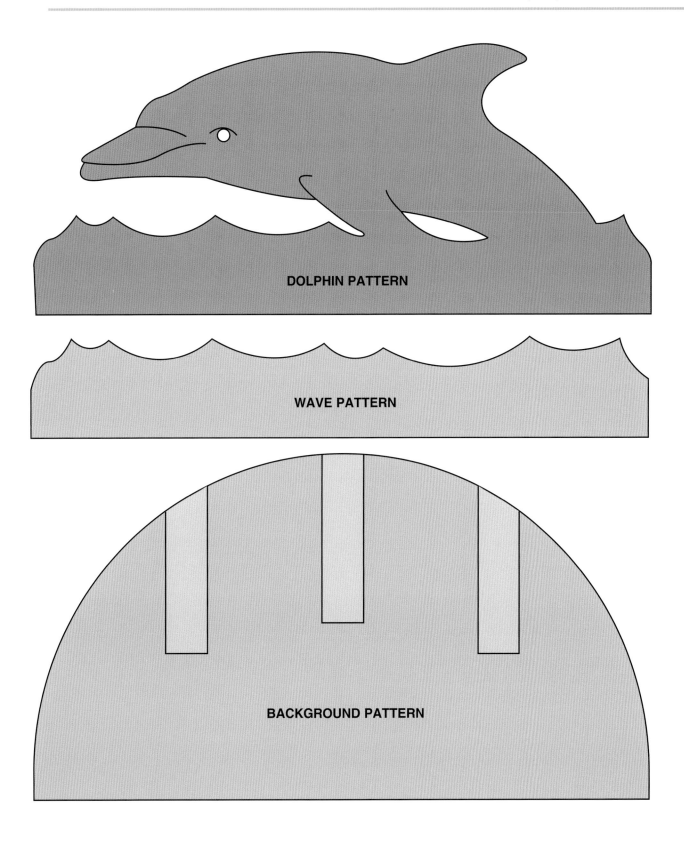

DOLPHIN PATTERN

WAVE PATTERN

BACKGROUND PATTERN

4

Patterns With Sharp Curves and Inside Cuts

For many of the projects in this chapter, you'll have to drill blade start holes that enable you to cut out areas within the pattern. It is suggested that you drill all the necessary blade start holes required in a pattern at the same time.

Tricky Clown Clock

MATERIALS LIST...✏

- ¼", ½"-, and ¾"-thick stock
- Paint
- ⅛"- and ¼"-diameter dowels
- ¾"-diameter clock movement

NOTE: The patterns for this project are shown at 80%. They should be enlarged to 125% for full size.

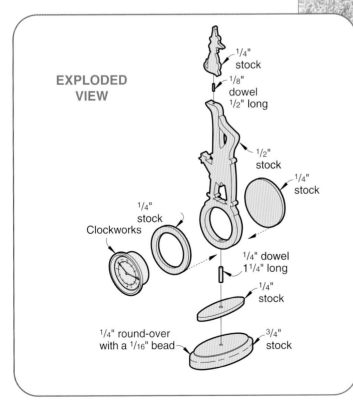

EXPLODED VIEW

¼" stock

⅛" dowel ½" long

½" stock

¼" stock

¼" stock

Clockworks

¼" dowel 1¼" long

¼" stock

¼" round-over with a ¹⁄₁₆" bead

¾" stock

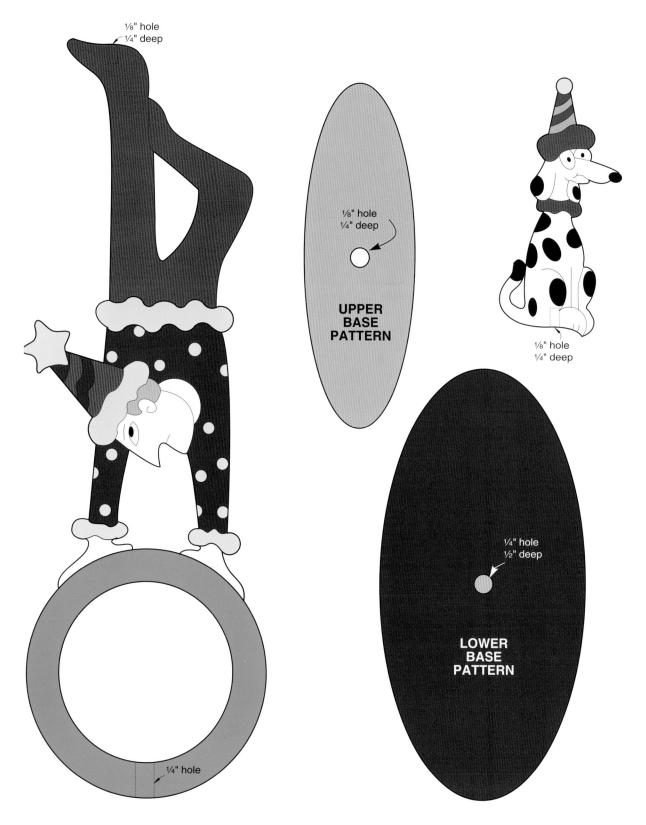

⅛" hole
¼" deep

⅛" hole
¼" deep

**UPPER
BASE
PATTERN**

⅛" hole
¼" deep

¼" hole
½" deep

**LOWER
BASE
PATTERN**

¼" hole

Picture-Perfect Jungle Hut

MATERIALS LIST...

- ¼"- and ¾"-thick stock
- Glass
- Small brads
- Flat-head wood screws
- Paint

NOTE: The patterns for this project are shown at 80%. They should be enlarged to 125% for full size.

Match grass pattern here

GRASS PATTERN

Match grass pattern here

GRASS PATTERN

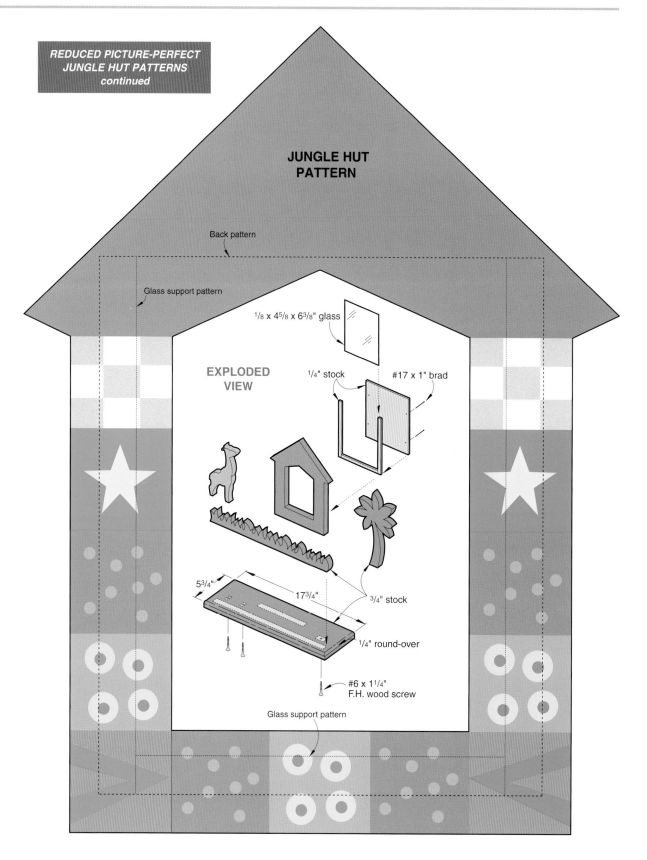

**JUNGLE HUT
PATTERN**

Back pattern

Glass support pattern

$^1/_8$ x $4^5/_8$ x $6^3/_8$" glass

**EXPLODED
VIEW**

$^1/_4$" stock

#17 x 1" brad

$^3/_4$" stock

$5^3/_4$"

$17^3/_4$"

$^1/_4$" round-over

#6 x $1^1/_4$"
F.H. wood screw

Glass support pattern

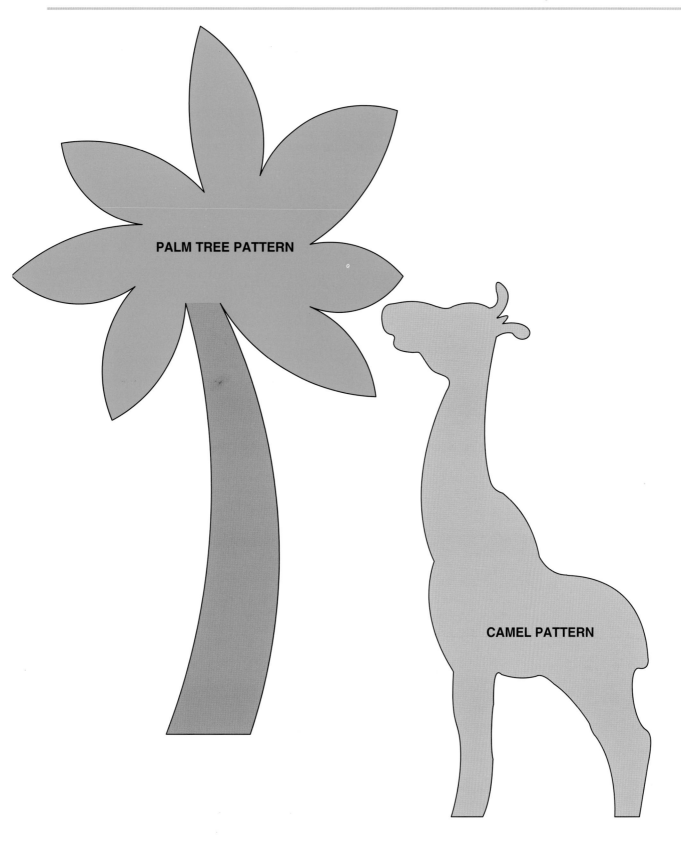

PALM TREE PATTERN

CAMEL PATTERN

Key-Clutter Cutter

MATERIALS LIST...

- ¾"-thick hardwood (walnut shown) for key board and hanger
- ¼"-thick hardwood (maple shown) for key fobs
- Glue or flat-head wood screws
- Clear finish
- Sawtooth hanger
- Wire or split rings for fob hangers

NOTE: The patterns for this project are shown at 60%. To make full size patterns, they must be enlarged to 167%.

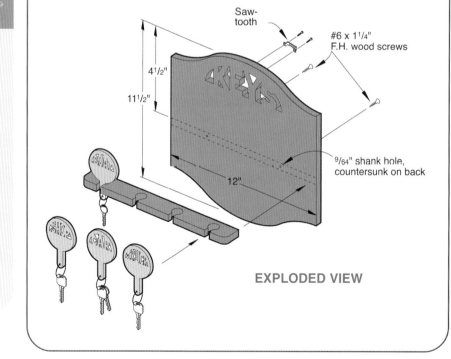

Saw-tooth

#6 x 1¼"
F.H. wood screws

4½"

11½"

12"

9/64" shank hole,
countersunk on back

EXPLODED VIEW

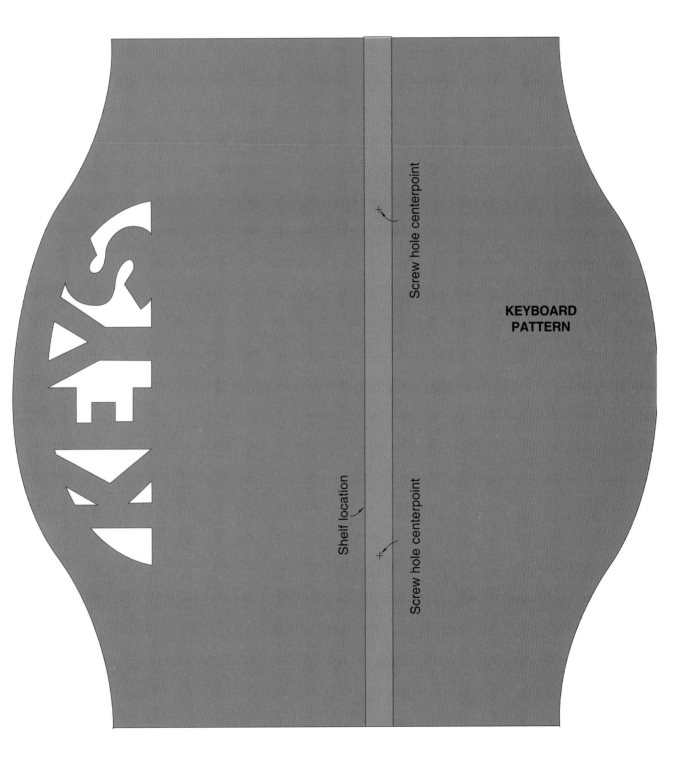

Screw hole centerpoint

KEYBOARD
PATTERN

Shelf location

Screw hole centerpoint

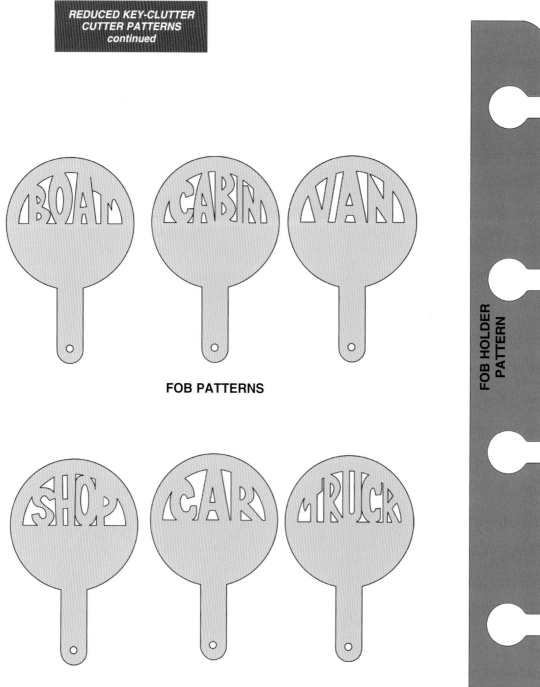

REDUCED KEY-CLUTTER CUTTER PATTERNS
continued

FOB PATTERNS

FOB PATTERNS

FOB HOLDER PATTERN

Breakfast Blooms Napkin Holder

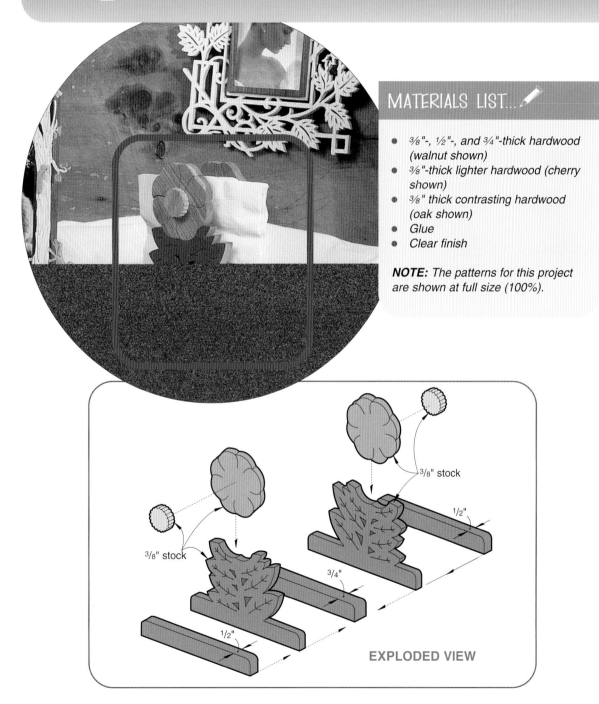

MATERIALS LIST... ✏️

- *⅜"-, ½"-, and ¾"-thick hardwood (walnut shown)*
- *⅜"-thick lighter hardwood (cherry shown)*
- *⅜" thick contrasting hardwood (oak shown)*
- *Glue*
- *Clear finish*

NOTE: *The patterns for this project are shown at full size (100%).*

³/₈" stock

³/₈" stock

1/2"

3/4"

1/2"

EXPLODED VIEW

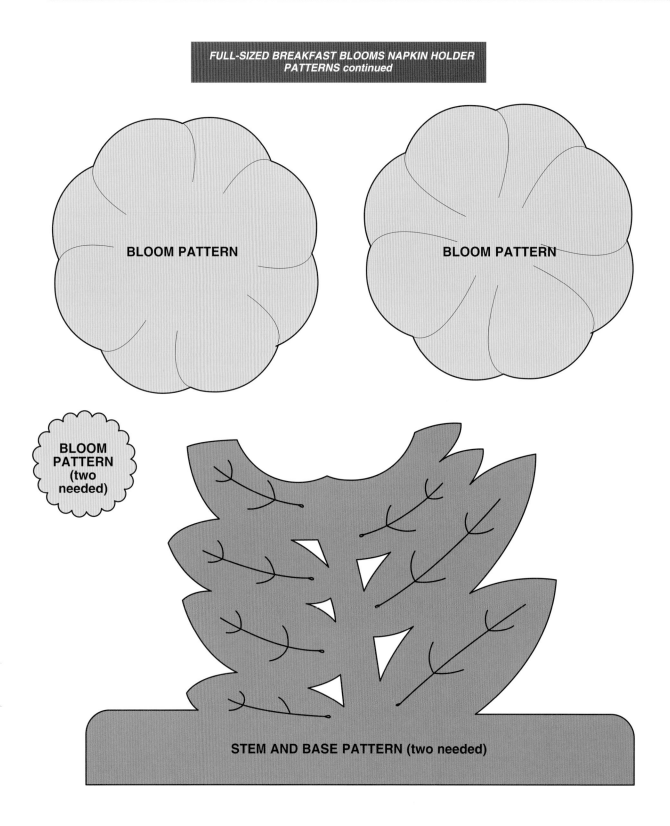

FULL-SIZED BREAKFAST BLOOMS NAPKIN HOLDER PATTERNS continued

BLOOM PATTERN

BLOOM PATTERN

BLOOM PATTERN (two needed)

STEM AND BASE PATTERN (two needed)

Looking for Moby

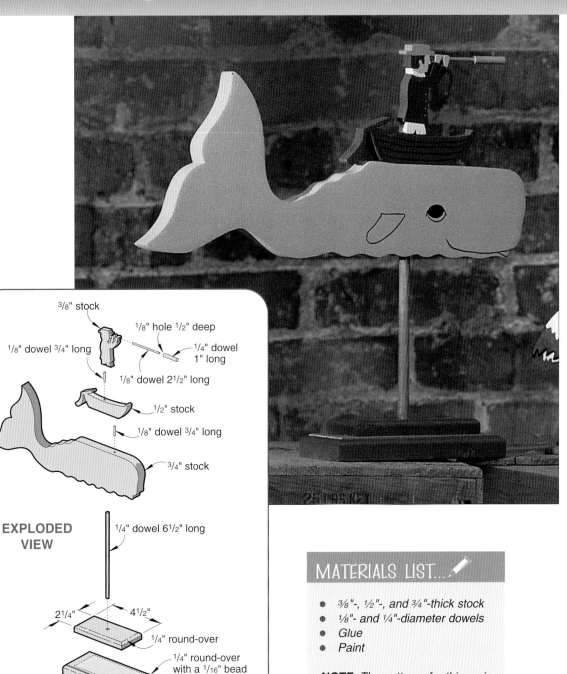

EXPLODED VIEW

3/8" stock

1/8" hole 1/2" deep

1/8" dowel 3/4" long

1/4" dowel 1" long

1/8" dowel 2 1/2" long

1/2" stock

1/8" dowel 3/4" long

3/4" stock

1/4" dowel 6 1/2" long

2 1/4"

4 1/2"

1/4" round-over

1/4" round-over with a 1/16" bead

6"

3"

MATERIALS LIST...

- 3/8"-, 1/2"-, and 3/4"-thick stock
- 1/8"- and 1/4"-diameter dowels
- Glue
- Paint

NOTE: The patterns for this project are shown at full size (100%).

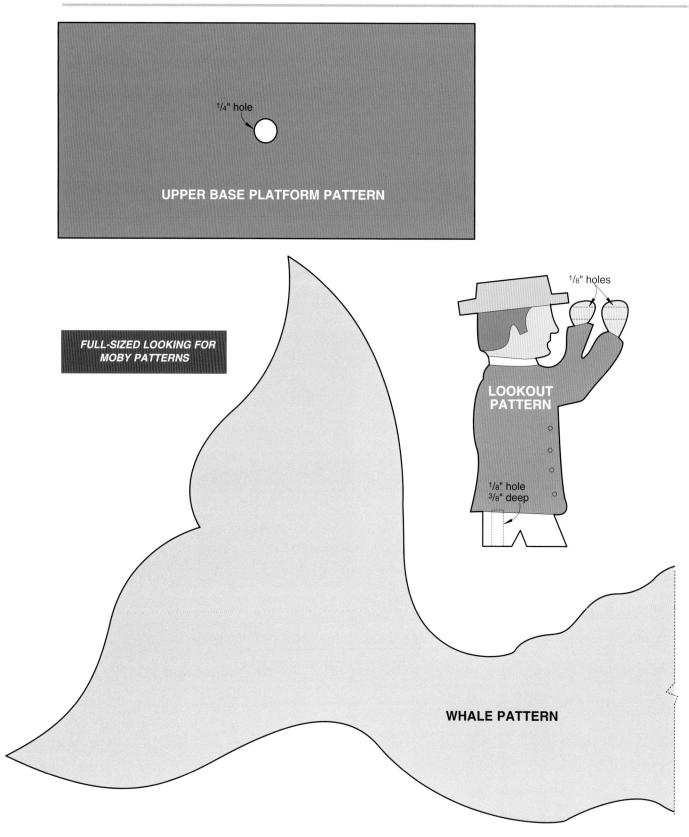

1/4" hole

UPPER BASE PLATFORM PATTERN

*FULL-SIZED LOOKING FOR
MOBY PATTERNS*

1/8" holes

**LOOKOUT
PATTERN**

1/8" hole
3/8" deep

WHALE PATTERN

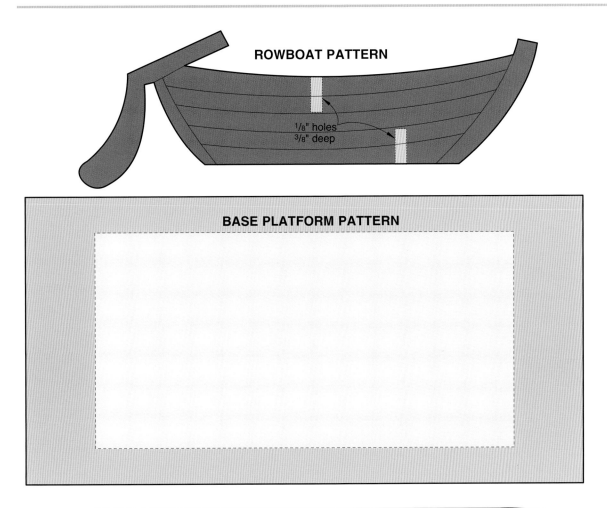

ROWBOAT PATTERN

1/8" holes
3/8" deep

BASE PLATFORM PATTERN

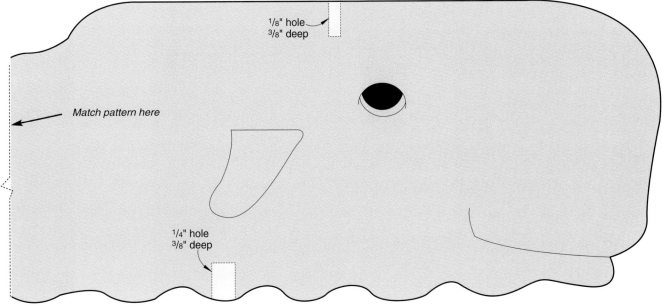

1/8" hole
3/8" deep

Match pattern here

1/4" hole
3/8" deep

Reindeer in Flight

Grace your mantel, sideboard, or table during the holidays with this three-dimensional winter scene. When the festivities are over, the scene disassembles for flat, compact storage.

MAKING THE REINDEER IN FLIGHT

1 Resaw and plane ¾"-thick maple stock to ¼" for the mountains (A, B, C). Make three copies of the mountain patterns. Note that all three mountains are on a combined pattern with different types of lines. Cut the mountain patterns close to the lines and adhere them to your stock with spray adhesive. Scrollsaw the mountains to shape. Drill blade start holes in the patterns' shaded areas, and saw them out.

2 Chuck a ⅛" brad-point drill bit in your drill press. Drill ⅛" holes ⅜" deep, where indicated on the mountain patterns, as shown below.

Using a fence to align the work, drill the ⅛" tree-mounting holes in the mountains, centered on their thickness.

EXPLODED VIEW

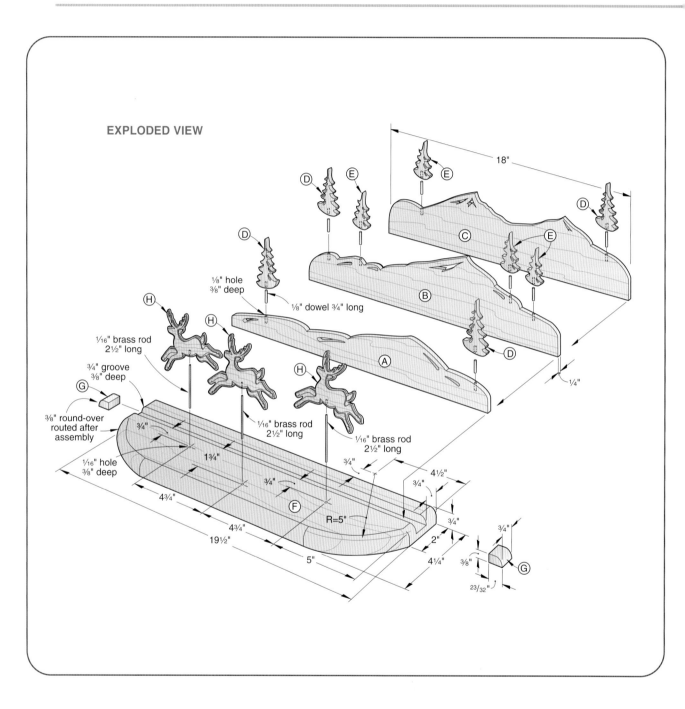

Glue the fillers in place, leaving ¹⁄₃₂" gaps at each end between the mountain and fillers. Remove the mountains, and wipe off any glue that squeezed out from the groove.

3 Resaw and plane ¾"-thick maple stock to ¼" thickness for the trees (D, E). Make four copies of each tree using the pattern, and adhere them to your ¼"-thick stock with spray adhesive. Drill blade start holes in the patterns' shaded areas, and saw them out. Scrollsaw the trees. Clamp the trees to your drill-press fence, and drill the ⅛" holes in their bottoms, where indicated on the pattern. Cut eight ¾"-long pieces of ⅛" dowel, and glue them into the holes.

4 Cut the base (F) to the size shown. Install a ¾" dado blade in your tablesaw, and cut a ⅜"-deep groove where shown in the Exploded View. Stack the three mountains together and check their fit in the groove. They should slip in and out of the groove with little play.

5 Drill the three ¹⁄₁₆" holes in the base, where shown. Draw the 5" radii at the base's ends, and bandsaw and sand them to the lines.

6 Cut a ⅜ × ¾ x8" blank in the fillers (G). Then cut off two 2"-long pieces. Center the mountains side-to-side in the groove. Glue the fillers in the groove, as shown in the photo above. Trim the fillers flush with the base, and rout the ⅜" round-over, as shown.

7 Make the three cherry reindeer (H). Drill ¹⁄₁₆" holes ⅜" deep, centered on the thickness of the bodies, where shown on the pattern.

76

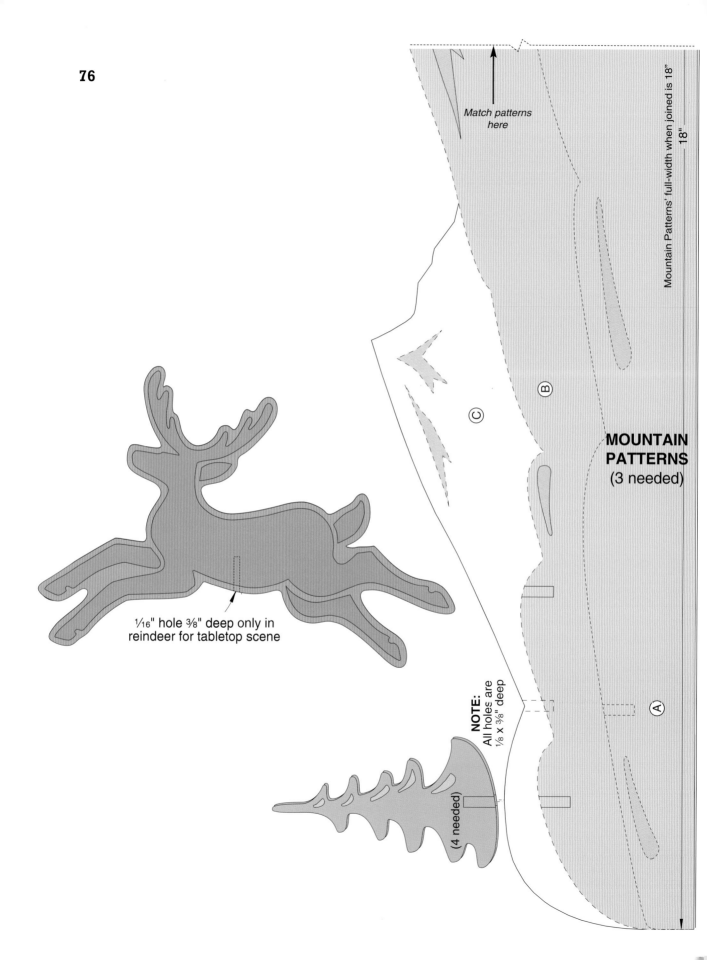

Match patterns here

Mountain Patterns' full-width when joined is 18"

18"

MOUNTAIN PATTERNS (3 needed)

Ⓒ

Ⓑ

Ⓐ

1/16" hole 3/8" deep only in reindeer for tabletop scene

NOTE: All holes are 1/8 x 3/8" deep

(4 needed)

8 Cut three 2½"-long pieces of ⅟₁₆" brass rod for the reindeer stands. Glue them into the reindeer's bodies.

9 Sand all the parts to 320 grit. Apply green aniline dye to the trees. Finish with three coats of aerosol satin lacquer. With the finish dry, position the mountains in the base's groove, and insert the tree's dowels in the mountains holes, where shown in the Exploded View on page 74. Insert the reindeer's rods in the base holes. Grasp the left-hand reindeer's brass rod just below its body with needle-nosed pliers, and bend the rod, angling the reindeer slightly downward. Repeat with a right-hand reindeer, but give it a slight upward angle.

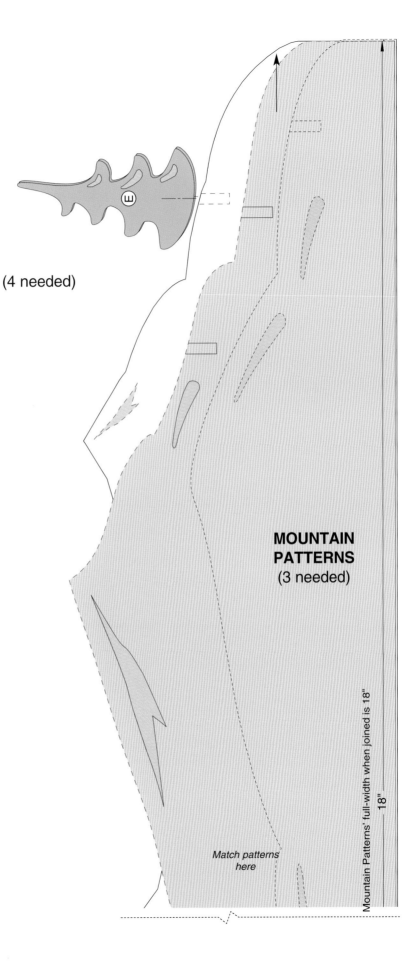

(4 needed)

MOUNTAIN PATTERNS
(3 needed)

Match patterns here

Mountain Patterns' full-width when joined is 18"

18"

Happy Holidays Tabletop Decoration

This festive rendition of the classic Christmas tree can be displayed on a mantel or as a table centerpiece.

MATERIALS LIST...✎

- ⅛"-thick birch plywood
- ¾"-thick stock (for candle supports)
- Glue
- Paint

NOTE: The patterns for this project are shown at 70%. For full size enlarge patterns to 143%

Note: Do not burn candles in wooden candle-holders. Add unlit candles for effect only!

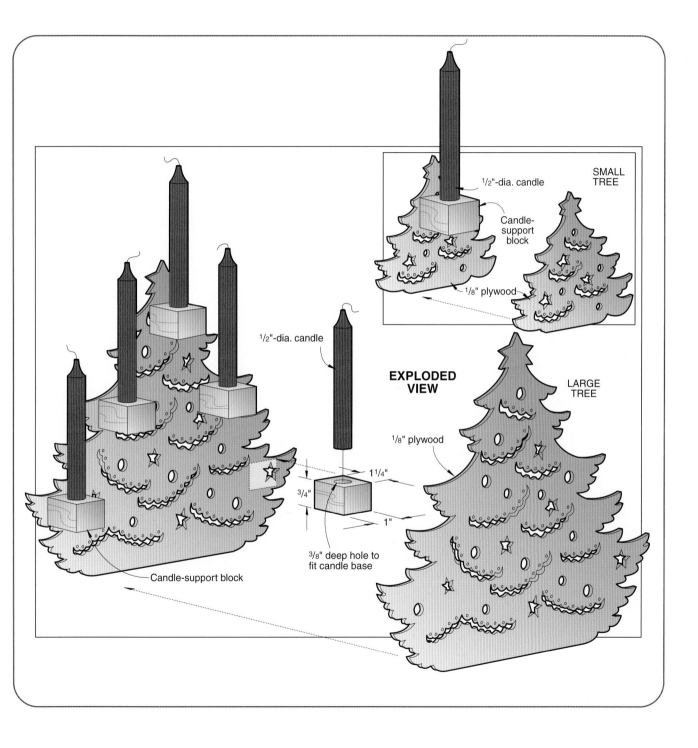

1/2"-dia. candle

SMALL TREE

Candle-support block

1/8" plywood

1/2"-dia. candle

EXPLODED VIEW

LARGE TREE

1/8" plywood

1 1/4"

3/4"

1"

3/8" deep hole to fit candle base

Candle-support block

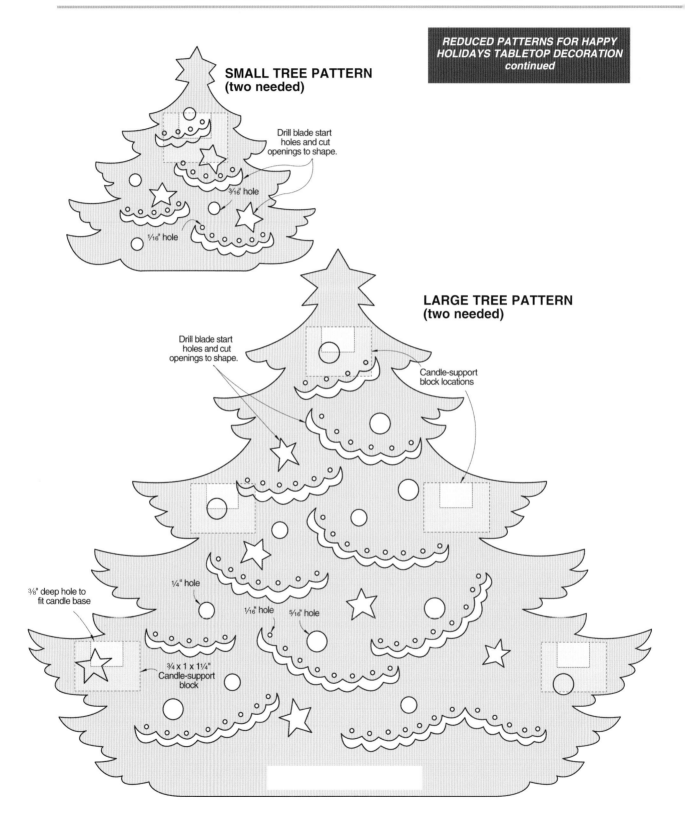

SMALL TREE PATTERN
(two needed)

Drill blade start holes and cut openings to shape.

³⁄₁₆" hole

¹⁄₁₆" hole

LARGE TREE PATTERN
(two needed)

Drill blade start holes and cut openings to shape.

Candle-support block locations

³⁄₈" deep hole to fit candle base

¼" hole

¹⁄₁₆" hole

⁵⁄₁₆" hole

¾ x 1 x 1¼"
Candle-support block

Bears Puzzle

This adorable, four-piece display puzzle can be made from scraps of any type of ¾"-thick wood (poplar was used for the puzzle shown here).

Scrollsaw down the center of the pattern lines to separate the bears and create their face, arm, and leg details.

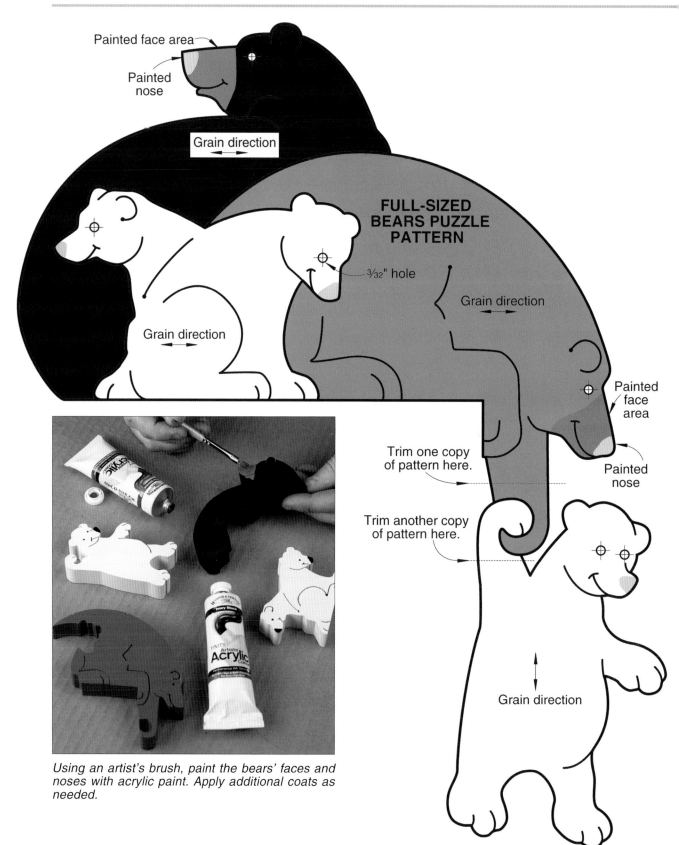

Painted face area

Painted nose

Grain direction

FULL-SIZED BEARS PUZZLE PATTERN

3/32" hole

Grain direction

Grain direction

Painted face area

Painted nose

Trim one copy of pattern here.

Trim another copy of pattern here.

Grain direction

Using an artist's brush, paint the bears' faces and noses with acrylic paint. Apply additional coats as needed.

Intermediate Patterns

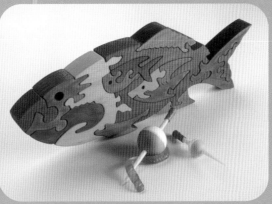

5

Patterns with Variety

If you're progressing through this book chapter by chapter, you've now arrived at the section where the majority of patterns demand combinations of the various cuts you've already performed. You'll also find it necessary to switch blades occasionally as each project's stock thickness requires.

Picture-Window Frame

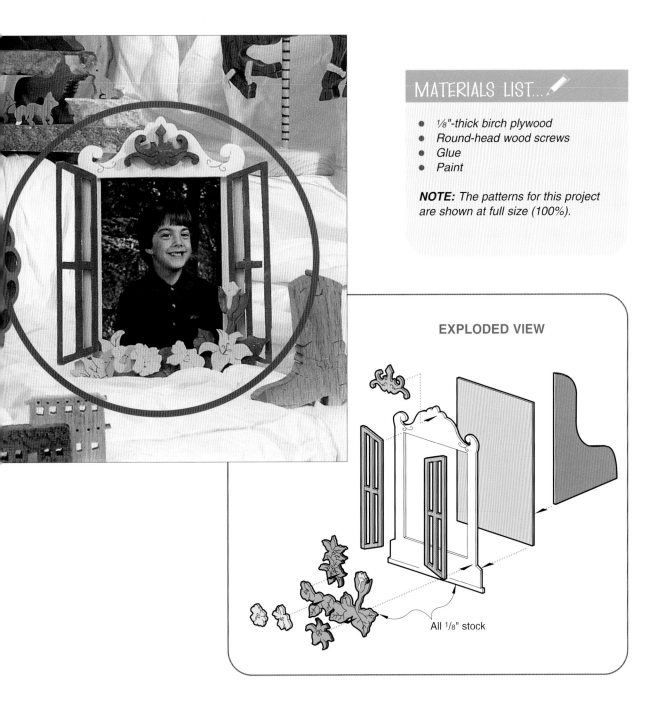

MATERIALS LIST...

- ⅛"-thick birch plywood
- Round-head wood screws
- Glue
- Paint

NOTE: The patterns for this project are shown at full size (100%).

EXPLODED VIEW

All ⅛" stock

FULL-SIZED PICTURE WINDOW PATTERNS

FLOWER
PATTERN

FLOWER
PATTERN

Back

FLOWER PATTERNS

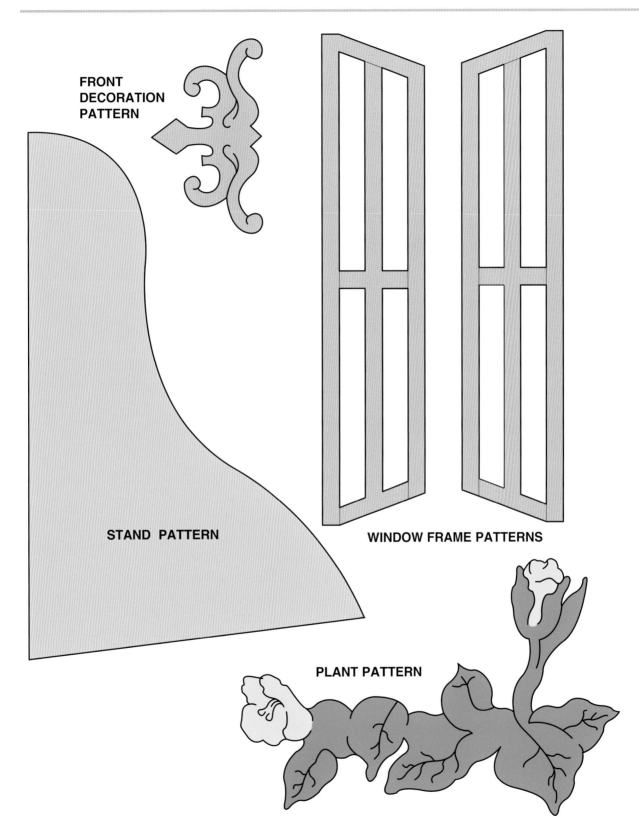

FRONT
DECORATION
PATTERN

STAND PATTERN

WINDOW FRAME PATTERNS

PLANT PATTERN

Tulip-Time Desk Box

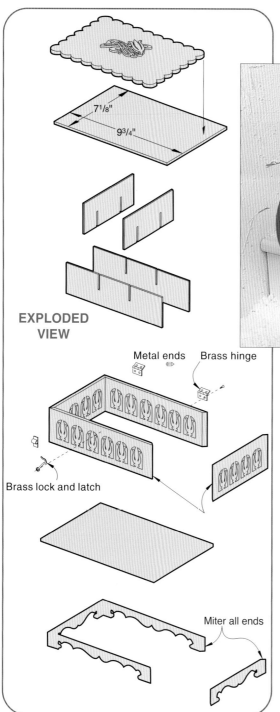

7¹/₈"

9³/₄"

EXPLODED VIEW

Metal ends   Brass hinge

Brass lock and latch

Miter all ends

MATERIALS LIST...

- ¼"-thick oak or walnut (for box parts)
- ⅛"-thick oak or walnut (for lid ornament)
- ⅛"thick oak, walnut, or birch plywood (for optional dividers)
- Glue
- Clear finish
- ¾" brass hinges

NOTE: The patterns for this project are shown at 60%. For full size, enlarge the patterns to 167%.

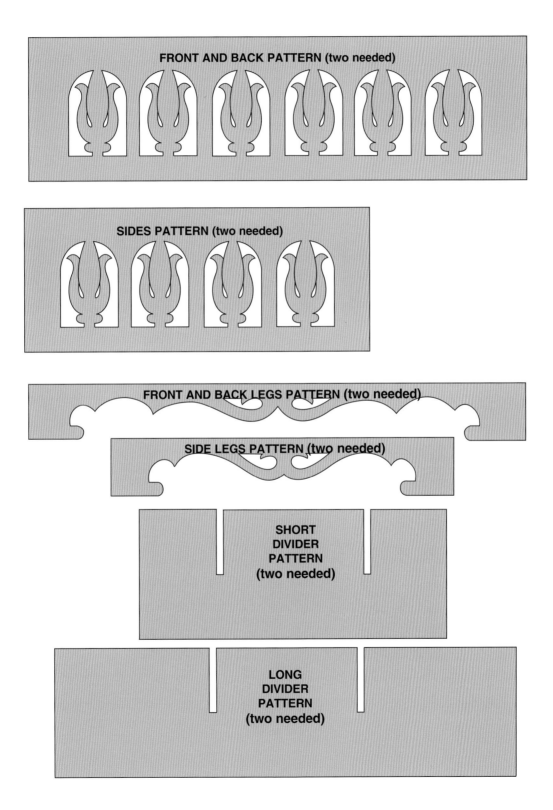

FRONT AND BACK PATTERN (two needed)

SIDES PATTERN (two needed)

FRONT AND BACK LEGS PATTERN (two needed)

SIDE LEGS PATTERN (two needed)

SHORT
DIVIDER
PATTERN
(two needed)

LONG
DIVIDER
PATTERN
(two needed)

**REDUCED
TULIP-TIME
DESK BOX
PATTERNS**
continued

LID ORNAMENT TOP PATTERN

TOP AND BASE PATTERN

Top-of-the-Morning Toast Rack

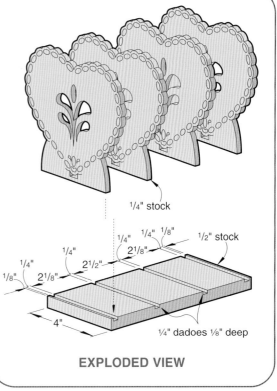

1/4" stock

EXPLODED VIEW

MATERIALS LIST...

- 1/4"- and 1/2"- thick walnut
- Glue
- Clear finish

NOTE: The pattern for this project is shown at full size (100%).

TOAST-HOLDER PATTERN (four needed)

Top-Notch Tray

MATERIALS LIST...

- ¼" thick walnut
- ¼" thick walnut plywood
- Glue
- Clear finish
- Brass corners

NOTE: *The patterns for this project are shown at 50%. For full size, enlarge to 200%.*

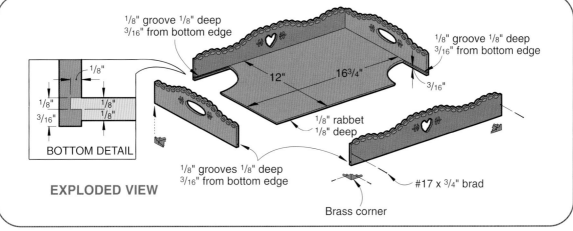

1/8" groove 1/8" deep
3/16" from bottom edge

1/8" groove 1/8" deep
3/16" from bottom edge

12" 16³/₄"

3/16"

1/8" rabbet
1/8" deep

1/8"

1/8" 1/8"

1/8" 1/8"

3/16"

BOTTOM DETAIL

EXPLODED VIEW

1/8" grooves 1/8" deep
3/16" from bottom edge

#17 x 3/4" brad

Brass corner

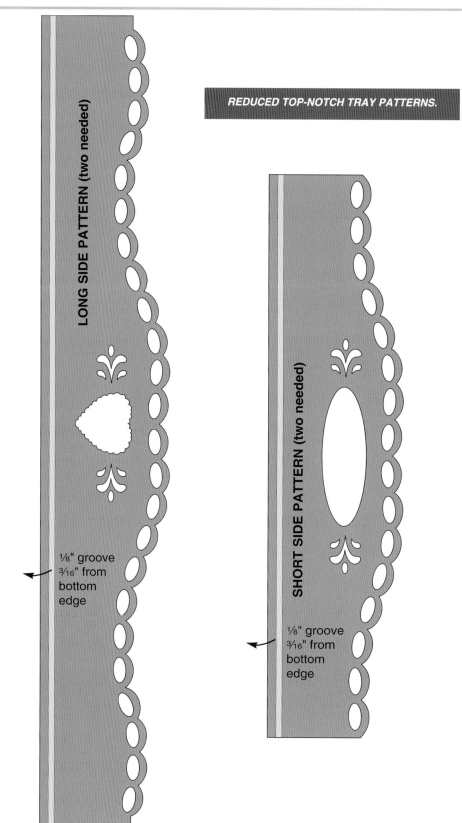

REDUCED TOP-NOTCH TRAY PATTERNS.

LONG SIDE PATTERN (two needed)

⅛" groove ³⁄₁₆" from bottom edge

SHORT SIDE PATTERN (two needed)

⅛" groove ³⁄₁₆" from bottom edge

Prehistoric Puzzlers

MATERIALS LIST....

- ¾"-thick stock
- Paint

NOTE: *The patterns for this project are shown at 50%. For full size, enlarge to 200%.*

MOUNTAIN PUZZLE

OCEAN PUZZLE

MOUNTAIN PATTERN

OCEAN PATTERN

OPTIONAL PUZZLE PATTERN

The Great Puzzle Fish

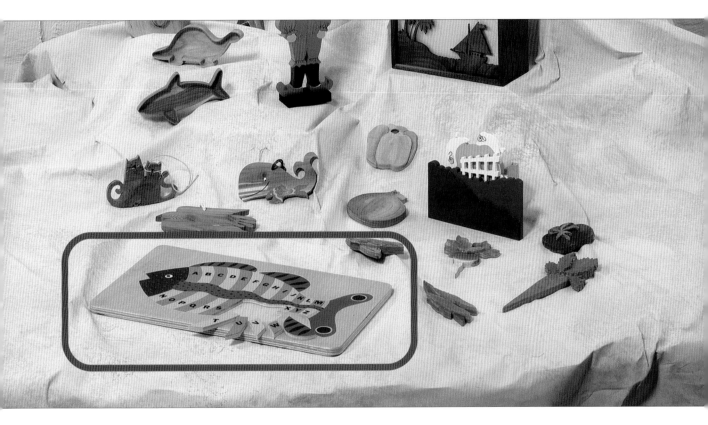

MATERIALS LIST...

- ¼"-thick birch plywood
- Paint
- Press-on letters (available at art-supply stores)

NOTE: The pattern for this project is shown at 55%. For full size, enlarge to 182%.

REDUCED
GREAT
PUZZLE
FISH
PATTERN

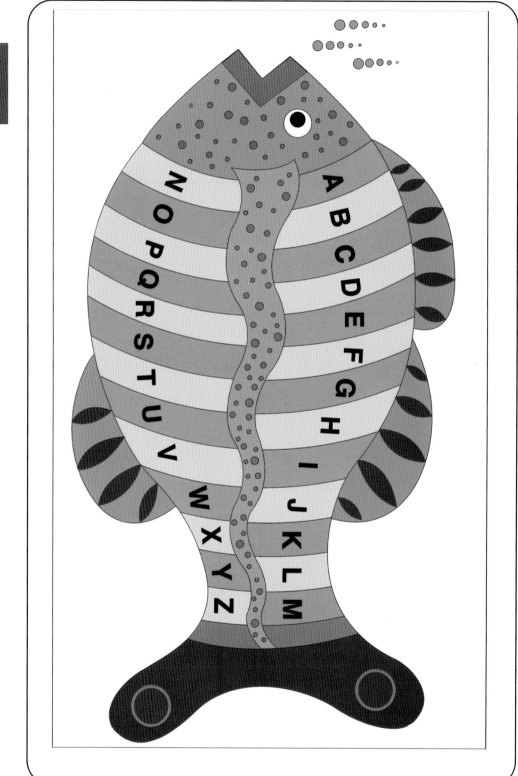

Dandy Desk Trays

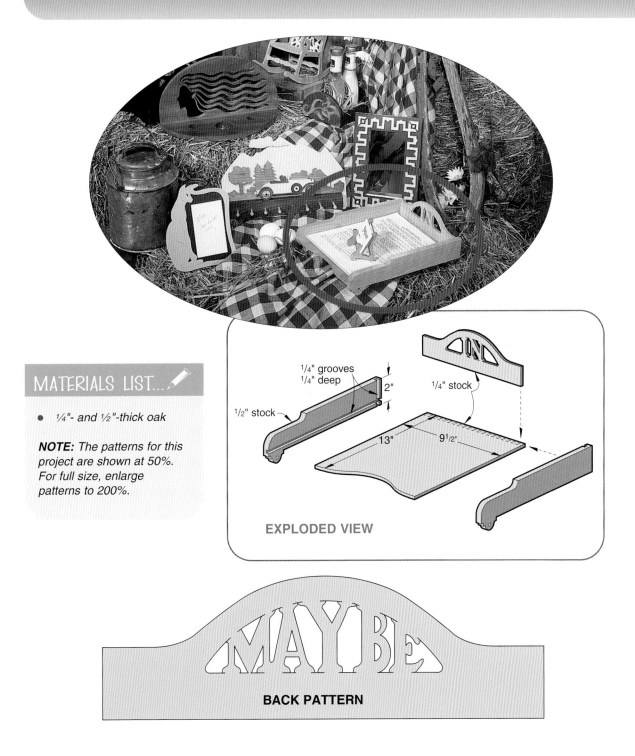

MATERIALS LIST...

- ¼"- and ½"-thick oak

NOTE: The patterns for this project are shown at 50%. For full size, enlarge patterns to 200%.

¼" grooves
¼" deep

2"

¼" stock

½" stock

13"

9½"

EXPLODED VIEW

BACK PATTERN

BOTTOM PANEL PATTERN

¼" grooves
¼" deep

SIDE PATTERN (two needed)

BACK PATTERN

BACK PATTERN

6

Patterns with Depth

Assuming that you've made some, if not all, of the projects on the preceding pages, you're well-prepared for the patterns on the following pages. A few require the attention and cutting skill of intermediate fretwork, popular during the Victorian era.

Lace-Edged Memento Box

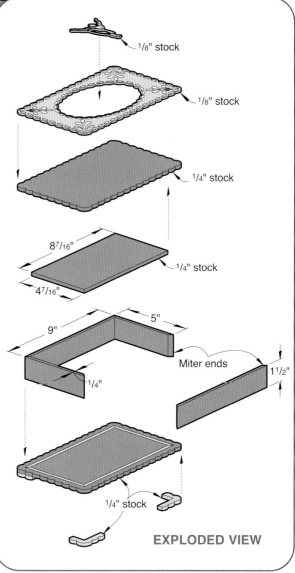

1/8" stock

1/8" stock

1/4" stock

8⁷/₁₆"

4⁷/₁₆"

1/4" stock

9"

5"

Miter ends

1/4"

1¹/₂"

1/4" stock

EXPLODED VIEW

MATERIALS LIST... ✎

- ¼"-thick walnut and ash
- Glue
- Clear finish

NOTE: The patterns for this project are shown at 85%. For full size, enlarge to 118%.

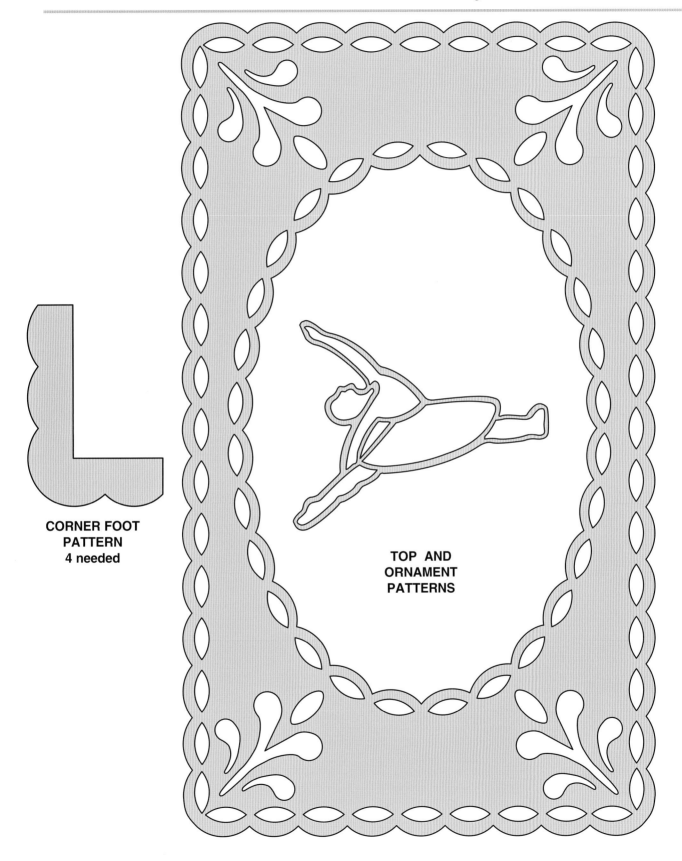

**CORNER FOOT
PATTERN
4 needed**

**TOP AND
ORNAMENT
PATTERNS**

BASE PATTERN

Hair-Care Appliance Holder

Here is a helpful household item that you can modify for your particular needs. The holes shown on the shelf pattern are typical for hair-care appliance holders, but you can change their locations and sizes to suit your brushes, dryers, and curling irons. You also can build a shelf without holes to hold other toiletries.

MATERIALS LIST...

- ½"-thick pine (or other stock)
- Clear finish

NOTE: *The patterns for this project are shown at 75%. For full size patterns, enlarge to 133%.*

EXPLODED VIEW

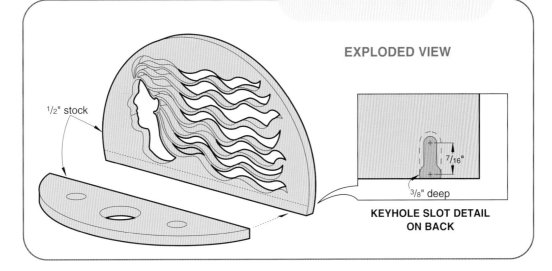

½" stock

7/16"

3/8" deep

KEYHOLE SLOT DETAIL ON BACK

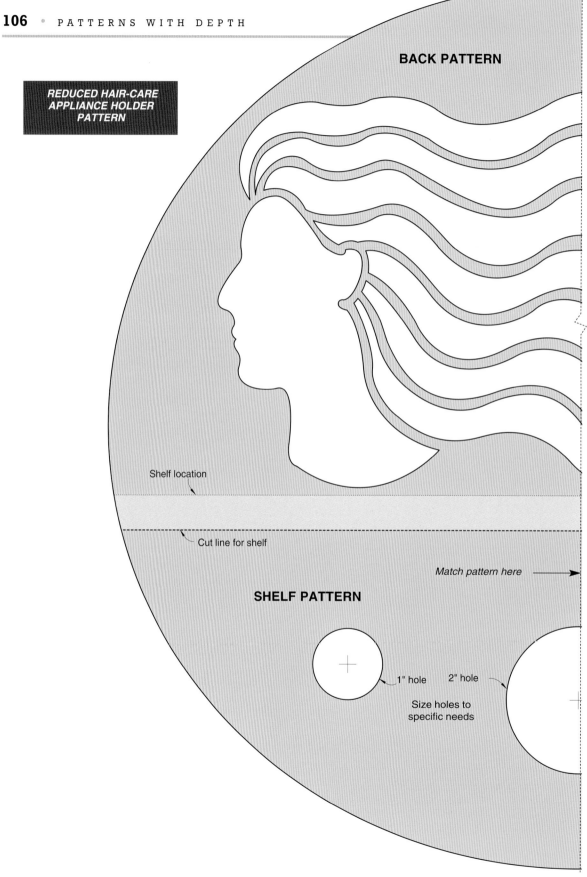

REDUCED HAIR-CARE APPLIANCE HOLDER PATTERN

BACK PATTERN

Shelf location

Cut line for shelf

Match pattern here →

SHELF PATTERN

1" hole   2" hole

Size holes to specific needs

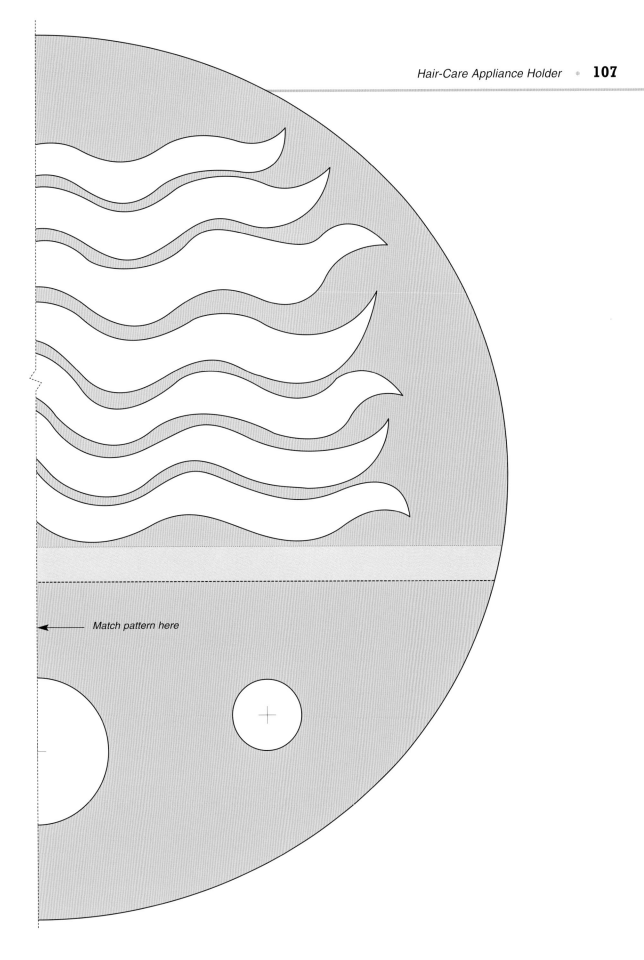

Match pattern here

Salad Servers with Drip Catcher

This eye-catching trio includes salad servers and a drip catcher that provides a place to lay down a tasting or stirring spoon without making a puddle on the countertop. The salad servers are made using compound cutting.

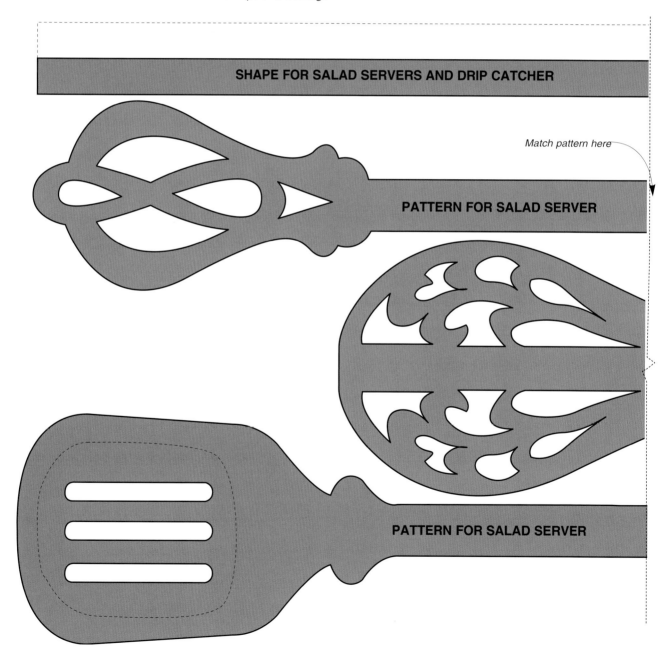

SHAPE FOR SALAD SERVERS AND DRIP CATCHER

Match pattern here

PATTERN FOR SALAD SERVER

PATTERN FOR SALAD SERVER

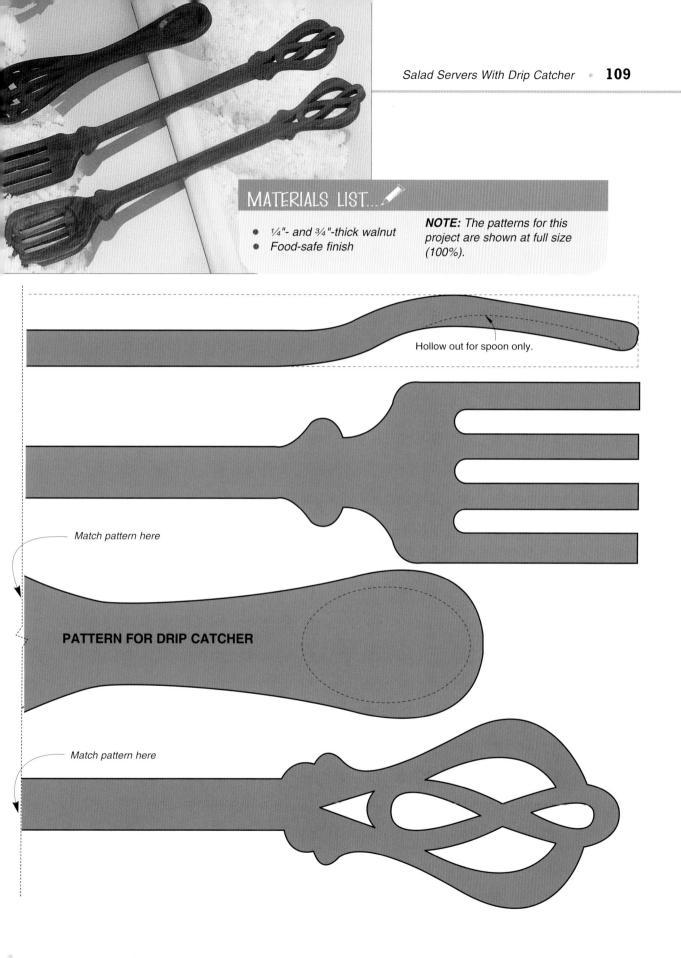

MATERIALS LIST...

- ¼"- and ¾"-thick walnut
- Food-safe finish

NOTE: *The patterns for this project are shown at full size (100%).*

Hollow out for spoon only.

Match pattern here

PATTERN FOR DRIP CATCHER

Match pattern here

Cowboy Curio Shelf

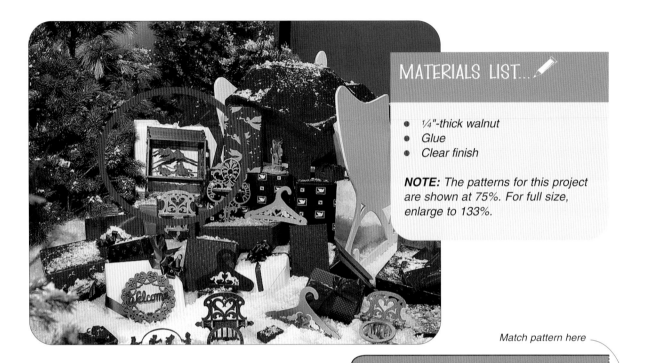

MATERIALS LIST...✎

- ¼"-thick walnut
- Glue
- Clear finish

NOTE: The patterns for this project are shown at 75%. For full size, enlarge to 133%.

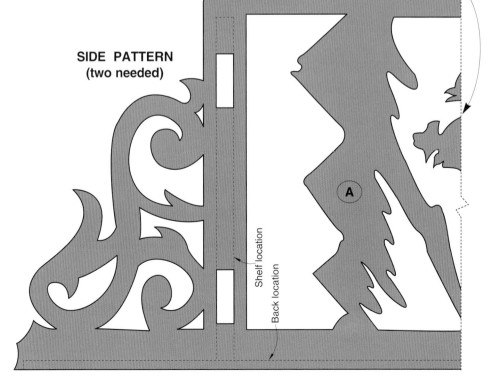

Match pattern here

SIDE PATTERN
(two needed)

A

Shelf location

Back location

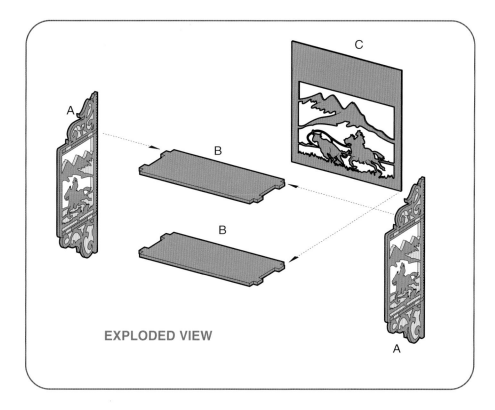

EXPLODED VIEW

Match pattern here

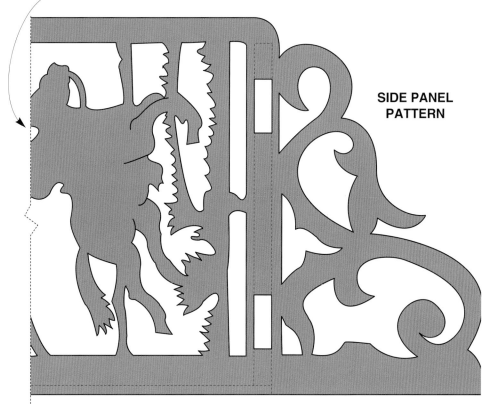

SIDE PANEL
PATTERN

Match pattern here

BACK PANEL PATTERN

C

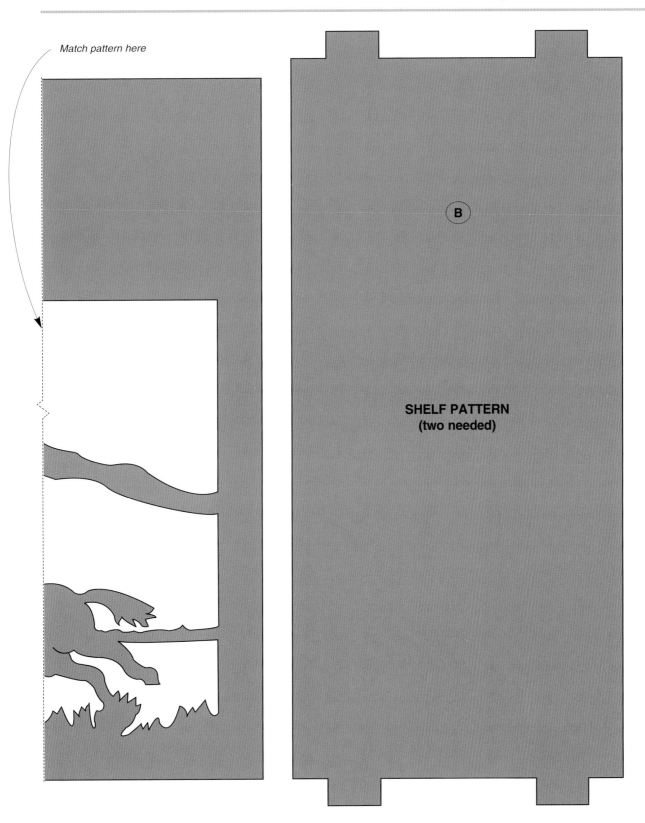

Match pattern here

B

SHELF PATTERN
(two needed)

One Fishy Puzzle

MATERIALS LIST...✏️

- ¾"-thick poplar or pine
- Aniline dyes or paint

NOTE: The patterns for this project are shown at full size (100%).

This fish puzzle has a clever design and eye-popping colors. Look closely and you'll spot not one but three bright fish going for a swim.

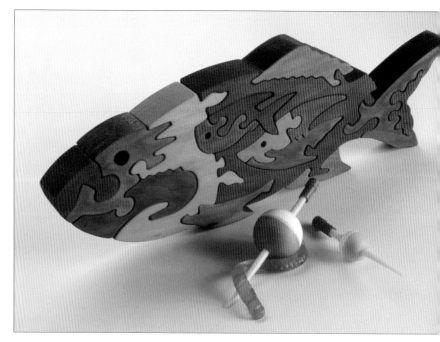

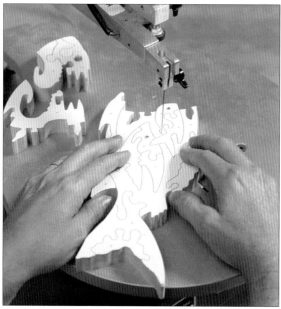

Working from the fish's mouth to its tail, cut out each puzzle piece as you come to it, sawing right down the middle of the pattern lines.

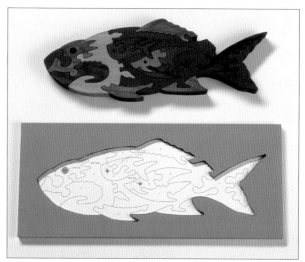

Fish puzzle frame and cutout.

KEY TO ANILINE DYE COLORS

1—Ruby
2—Green Peacock
3—Green Peacock Blue
4—Lemon Yellow
5—Brilliant Scarlet
6—Orange
7—Violet
8—Golden Yellow
9—Magenta

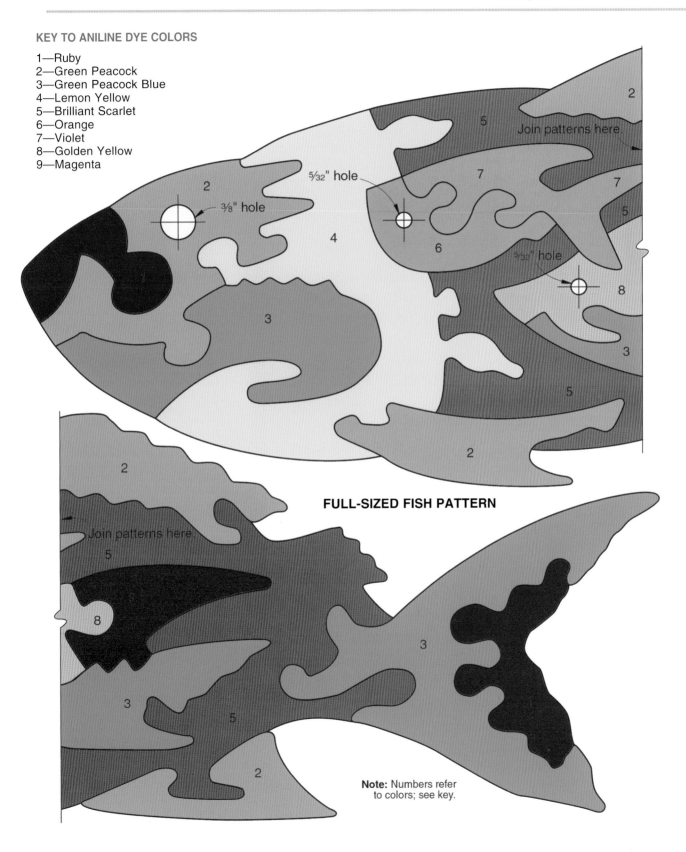

FULL-SIZED FISH PATTERN

Note: Numbers refer to colors; see key.

Safari Puzzle

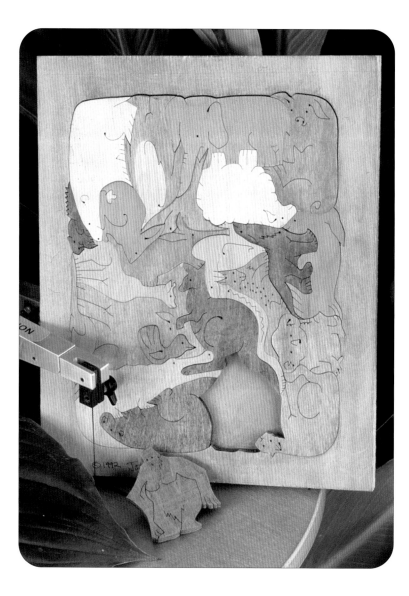

MATERIALS LIST....✎

- Two 8½ x 10" pieces of ¼"-thick birch plywood
- Paint

NOTE: The pattern for this project is shown at full size (100%.)

COLOR GUIDELINES

Pickling gels, gel stains, and acrylic colors were used for the following colors, as indicated in the drawing:

BL—Navy blue
BU—Burgundy
CG—Cactus green
CH—Cherry
DW—Driftwood
GO—Goldenrod
MG—Mahogany
ML—Maple
MW—Modern walnut
OR—Ceramcoat orange
   mixed 50/50 with
   neutral gcl
RP—Rose pink
SO—Sunset orange
WH—Desert white.

The back and frame were stained with a 50/50 mix of Ceramcoat black green and neutral gel. Wipe on desert white and wipe it off again to glaze the frame and back.

FULL-SIZED PATTERN

Snowman

Sand the contours and round over the edges of the Snowman to create a three-dimentional appearance.

FULL-SIZED SNOWMAN PATTERN

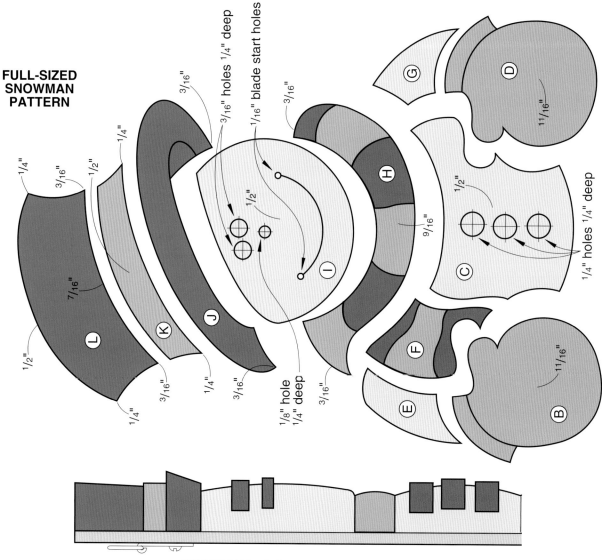

3/16" holes 1/4" deep

1/16" blade start holes

1/8" hole 1/4" deep

1/4" holes 1/4" deep

SNOWMAN—SIDE VIEW SECTION

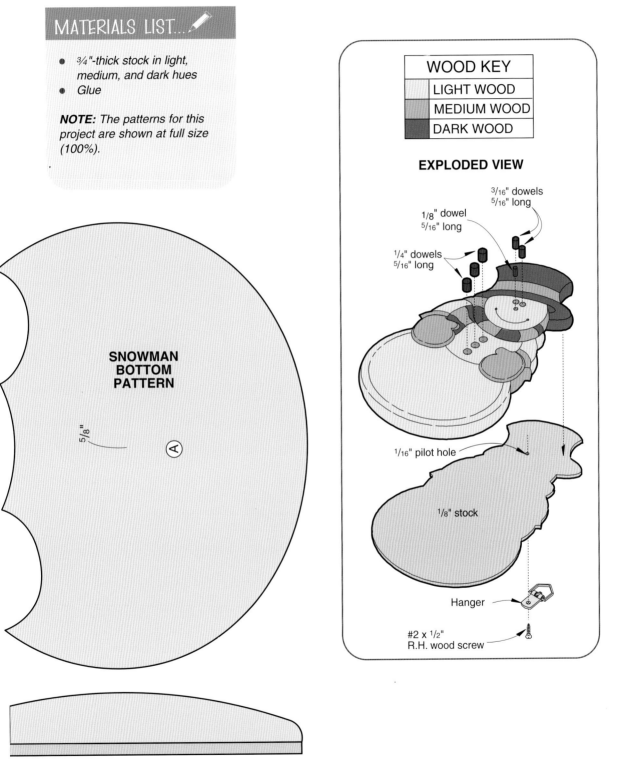

MATERIALS LIST...

- ¾"-thick stock in light, medium, and dark hues
- Glue

NOTE: *The patterns for this project are shown at full size (100%).*

WOOD KEY
LIGHT WOOD
MEDIUM WOOD
DARK WOOD

EXPLODED VIEW

3/16" dowels
5/16" long

1/8" dowel
5/16" long

1/4" dowels
5/16" long

1/16" pilot hole

1/8" stock

Hanger

#2 x 1/2"
R.H. wood screw

**SNOWMAN
BOTTOM
PATTERN**

5/8"

Ⓐ

SNOWMAN—SIDE VIEW SECTION

7

Time is of the Essence

Clocks have always been popular scrollsaw projects. In this chapter, you'll find four unique and vastly different clock projects, each providing you with hours of scrollsawing pleasure.

Time-of-the-Dinosaurs Clock

MAKING THE DINOSAURS CLOCK

1 Photocopy the full-sized patterns. Adhere them to ⅛" Baltic birch plywood.

2 Cut out all parts in numerical order. A No. 2 blade handles the fine cutting.

3 Cut out each part, sawing into each interior detail line as you come to it. Take care not to cut beyond the end of any interior pattern line. When you reach the end of a stopped line, back the blade out with the saw running.

4 Begin cutting the large dinosaur (No. 6) where indicated on the pattern. Cut inward from there to the eye, back out, and saw clockwise around the outside pattern line. Cut five spacers from the ⅛" plywood: two of them 1½" in diameter, two 1", and one ⁵⁄₁₆".

MATERIALS LIST...

- ⅛"-thick birch plywood
- ⅝"-thick walnut
- Clear finish
- Glue
- Quartz clock movement
  Note: Clock movements are avilable through catalogues and online suppliers.

NOTE: *The patterns for this project are shown at full size(100%).*

5 Enlarge the clock body at 166 percent. Then enlarge the enlargement at 166 percent, and affix it to ¾ x 9 x 13" walnut stock.

6 Fit your scrollsaw with a heavier blade and tilt the table to 30°. Saw around the outside red pattern line first, keeping the clock body on the high side of the saw table. Then cut out the center of the body, following the blue line. Notice the different starting points, depending on your saw table's tilt direction. Keep the cutout part on the low side of the table.

7 Glue the center piece to the back of the U-shaped part. Drill a 5/16" hole for the clock movement where shown.

8 Assemble the parts in numerical order. First, position the left side tree (part 1) where shown jon page 136. Then glue the large spaces to the back of part 2, and place it where shown. When it is properly positioned, glue the parts into place. Glue parts 3, 4, and 5 onto part 2, referring to the photograph for positioning.

Part 6 slightly overlaps part 3, and part 7 overlaps parts 4 and 5. Refer to the photograph as you assemble the remaining parts.

Attach the clock face numbers and markers. Then install the clock movement and hands.

CLOCK BODY

Cutting instructions for the Time-of-the-Dinosaurs clock.

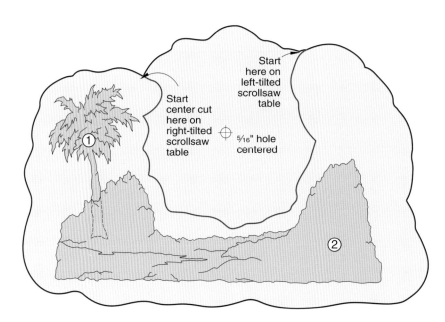

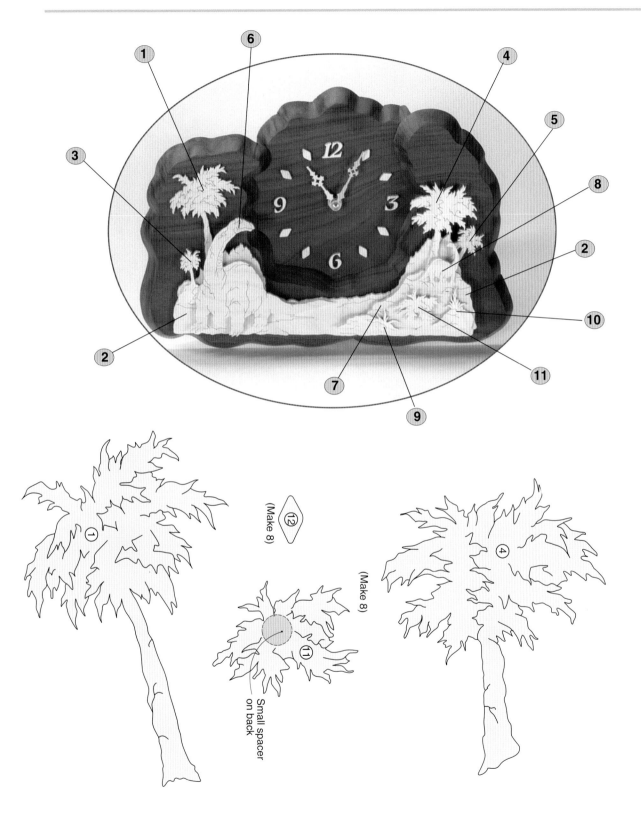

FULL-SIZED TIME-OF-THE-DINOSAURS CLOCK PATTERNS continued

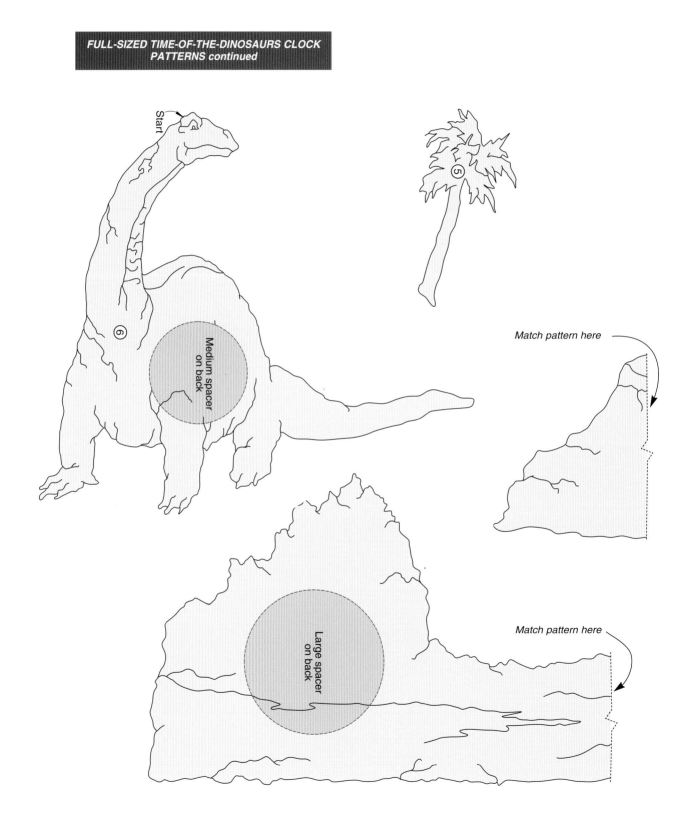

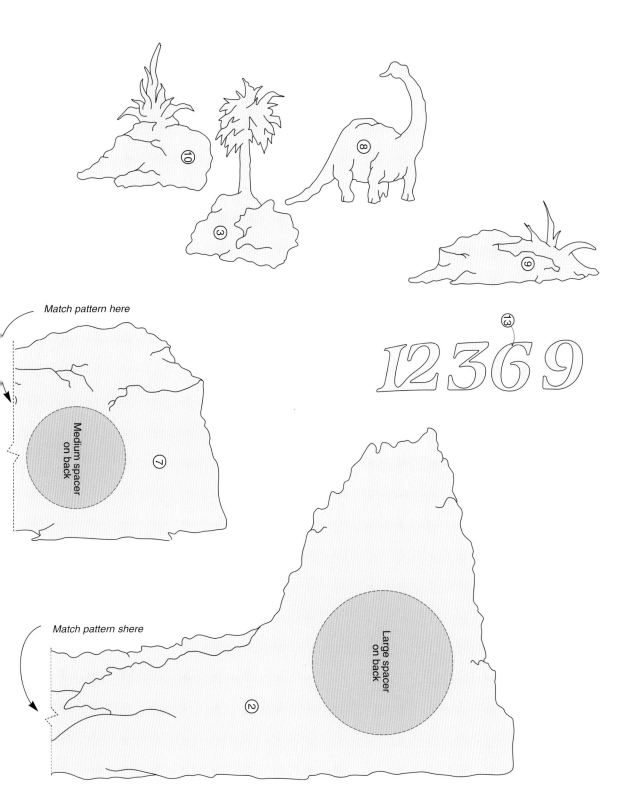

Match pattern here

Medium spacer on back

Match pattern shere

Large spacer on back

Old Oaken Clock

MATERIALS LIST... ✎

- ¼ x 8 x 8"-thick oak (part A)
- ½ x 8 x 8"-thick oak (part B)
- ⅜ x 8 x 8" piece of scrapwood (as a clamp pad)
- ⅜"-diameter dowels
- ⅜"-diameter oak buttons
- Glue
- Clear finish
- Quartz clock movement

NOTE: The pattern for this project is shown at 75%.
For full size patterns, enlarge to 133%.

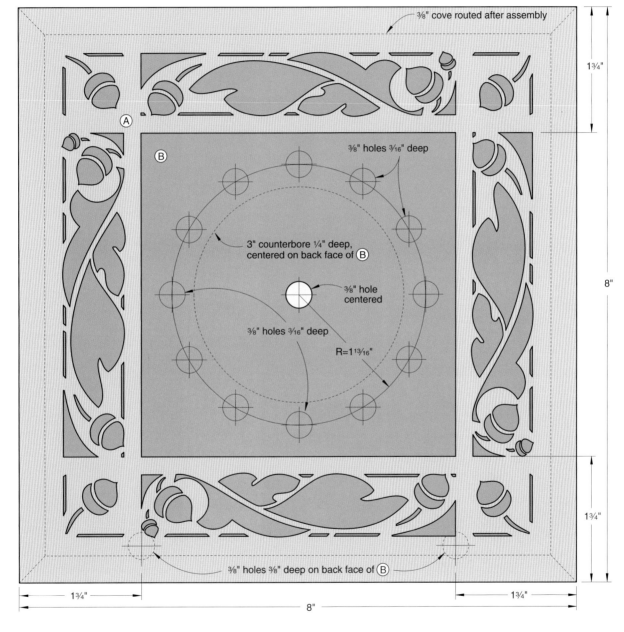

³⁄₈" cove routed after assembly

1³⁄₄"

8"

Ⓐ

Ⓑ

³⁄₈" holes ³⁄₁₆" deep

3" counterbore ¼" deep,
centered on back face of Ⓑ

³⁄₈" hole
centered

³⁄₈" holes ³⁄₁₆" deep

R=1¹³⁄₁₆"

³⁄₈" holes ³⁄₈" deep on back face of Ⓑ

1³⁄₄"

1³⁄₄"

8"

1³⁄₄"

CLOCK FACE PATTERN

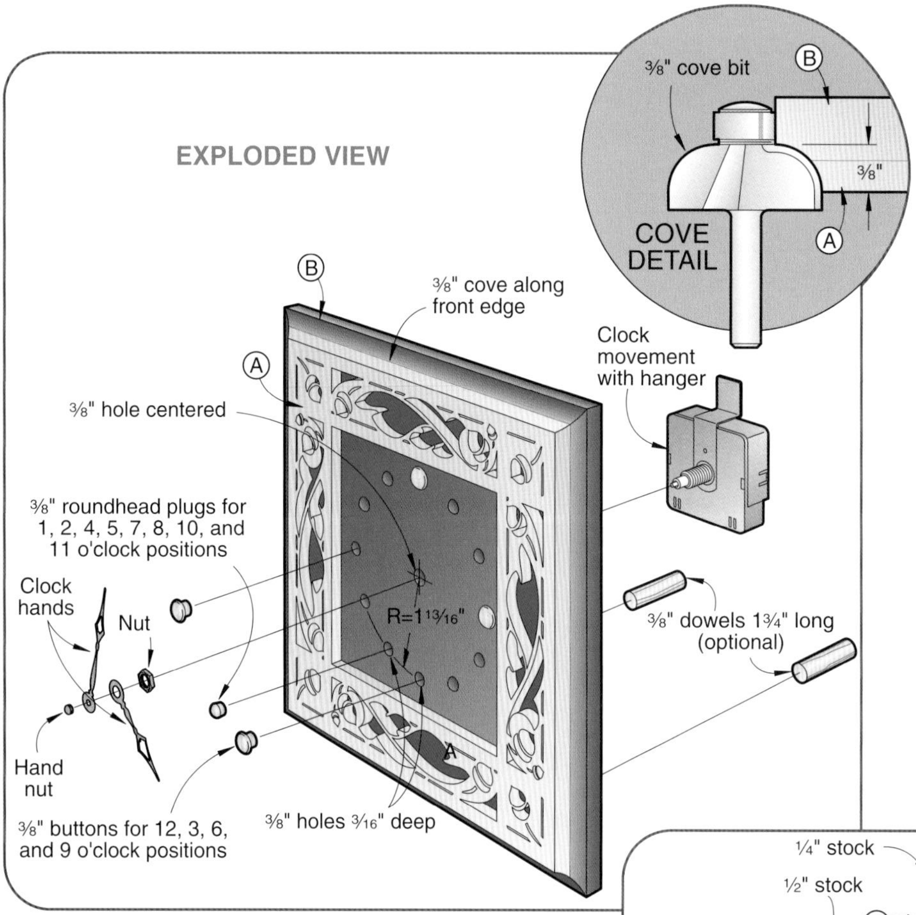
EXPLODED VIEW
COVE DETAIL
3/8" cove bit
3/8"
B
A
3/8" cove along front edge
3/8" hole centered
3/8" roundhead plugs for 1, 2, 4, 5, 7, 8, 10, and 11 o'clock positions
Clock hands
Nut
Hand nut
3/8" buttons for 12, 3, 6, and 9 o'clock positions
3/8" holes 3/16" deep
R=1 13/16"
Clock movement with hanger
3/8" dowels 1 3/4" long (optional)

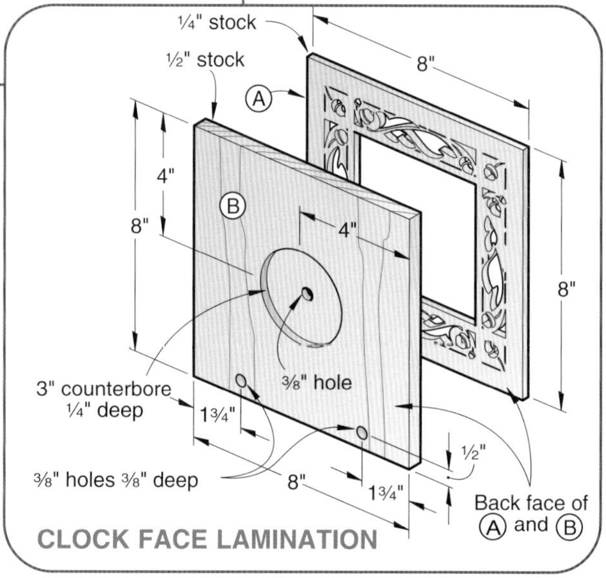
1/4" stock
1/2" stock
8"
4"
8"
4"
8"
3" counterbore 1/4" deep
3/8" hole
1 3/4"
3/8" holes 3/8" deep
8"
1 3/4"
1/2"
Back face of A and B
CLOCK FACE LAMINATION

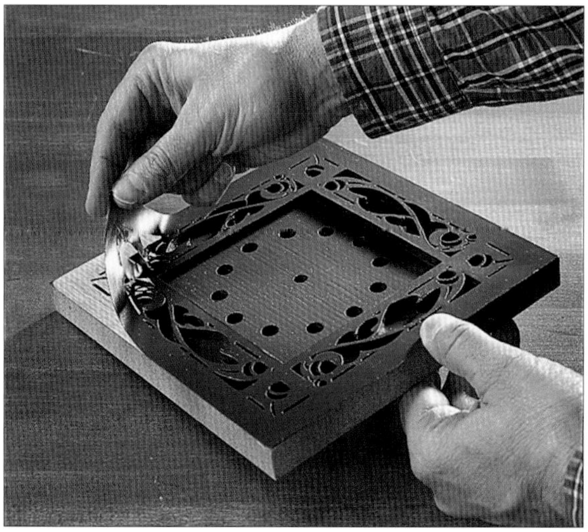

The pattern masks the fretwork for painting after scroll-sawing. The pattern is easier to remove after painting if you lacquer the wood surface first.

Towering Timepiece

A desk clock featuring New York City's Chrysler Building, one of American architecture's greatest achievements.

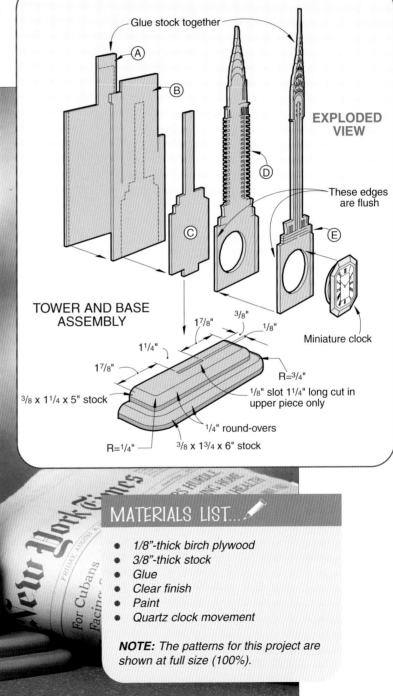

Glue stock together

A

B

EXPLODED VIEW

D

These edges are flush

E

C

Miniature clock

TOWER AND BASE ASSEMBLY

1⁷⁄₈"

3⁄₈"

1⁄₈"

1¼"

1⁷⁄₈"

R=³⁄₄"

³⁄₈ x 1¼ x 5" stock

¹⁄₈" slot 1¼" long cut in upper piece only

¼" round-overs

R=¼"

³⁄₈ x 1³⁄₄ x 6" stock

MATERIALS LIST...

- 1/8"-thick birch plywood
- 3/8"-thick stock
- Glue
- Clear finish
- Paint
- Quartz clock movement

NOTE: *The patterns for this project are shown at full size (100%).*

FULL-SIZED TOWERING TIMEPIECE PATTERNS

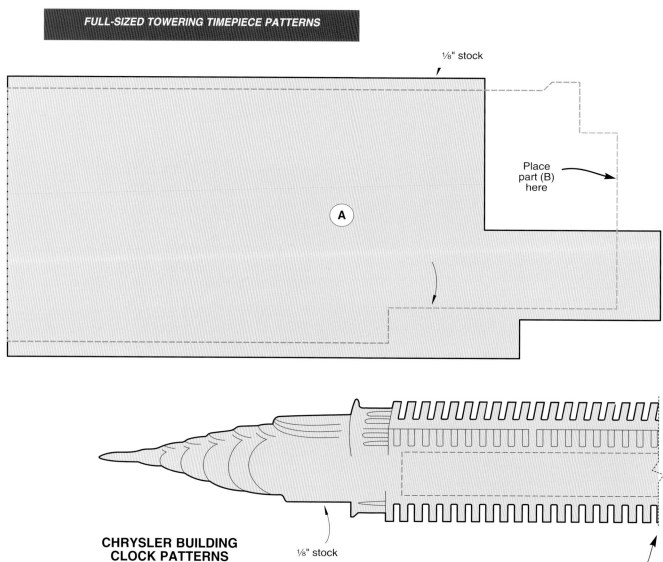

⅛" stock

Place
part (B)
here

A

**CHRYSLER BUILDING
CLOCK PATTERNS**

⅛" stock

Match patterns here

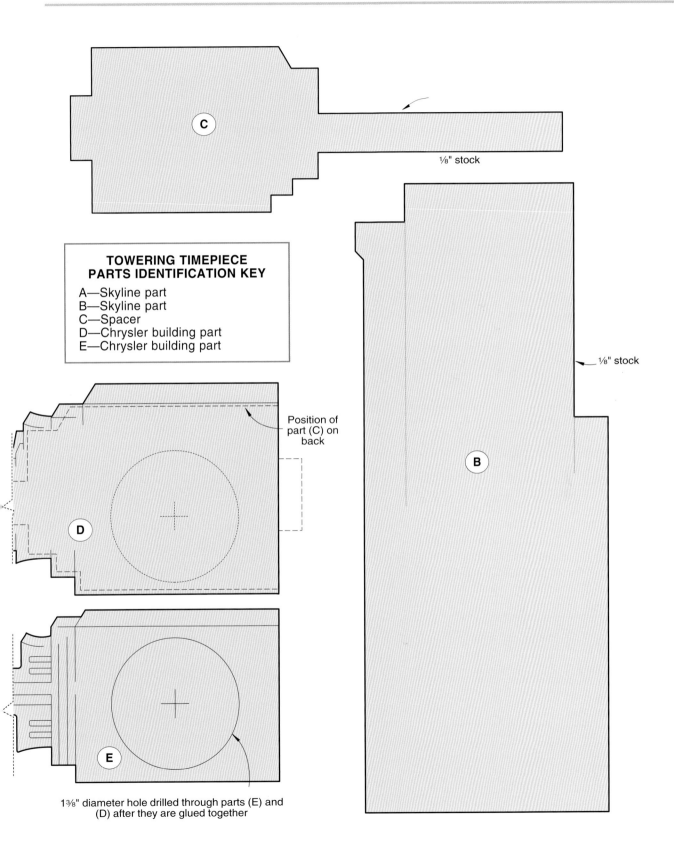

**TOWERING TIMEPIECE
PARTS IDENTIFICATION KEY**

A—Skyline part
B—Skyline part
C—Spacer
D—Chrysler building part
E—Chrysler building part

⅛" stock

⅛" stock

Position of
part (C) on
back

1⅜" diameter hole drilled through parts (E) and
(D) after they are glued together

Wetland Silhouette Clock

MATERIALS LIST...

- ¼"-thick walnut
- ¼"-thick birch plywood
- ¾"-thick birch
- Glue
- Clear finish
- Clock movement with hands

NOTE: The patterns for this project are shown at full size (100%).

EXPLODED VIEW

3/4"

1/4"

2¼"

B

¼" groove
3/8" deep

C

A

14¼"

6"

Wooden clock hands
(glued onto existing metal hands)

5/16" holes

D

Clock
movement

Nut

B

Miter corners
of frame

7½"

3¼"

3"

6"

Finish nut

Center numbers on hole centerpoint

Wetland Silhouette Clock Parts Identification Key

A—Sides
B—Ends
C—Front
D—Face

CLOCK HANDS PATTERNS

123456780
FULL-SIZED CLOCK NUMBERS

FULL-SIZED HERON PATTERN

Note: This pattern must be extended to an overall length of 11½" to allow space for the clock-face below.

Overall length 11³/₈"

Ⓓ

6"

8

More Challenging Patterns

Amazed so far by what you can accomplish with a scrollsaw? You'll be even more impressed with the bevy of patterns in this chapter. They'll provide new challenges to your scrollsawing skills.

Picture-Perfect Panda

MATERIALS LIST...

- *⅛"-thick birch plywood*
- *¾"-thick cedar (for back)*
- *Glue*
- *Clear finish*
- *⅛"-thick birch plywood or posterboard*
- *acrylic paints, water colors, or a clear finish*
- *fishing line or heavy thread*

NOTE: *The patterns for this project are shown at full size (100%).*

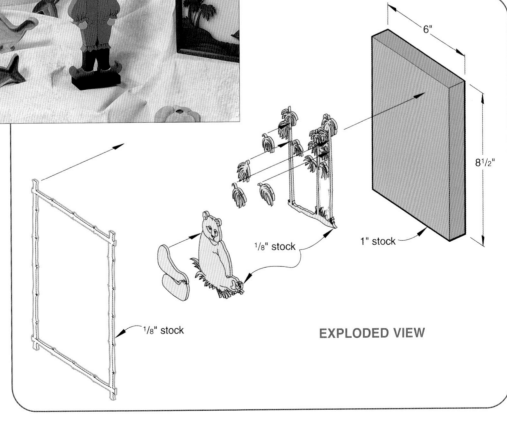

6"

8¹/₂"

¹/₈" stock

1" stock

¹/₈" stock

¹/₈" stock

EXPLODED VIEW

Match pattern here

Match pattern here

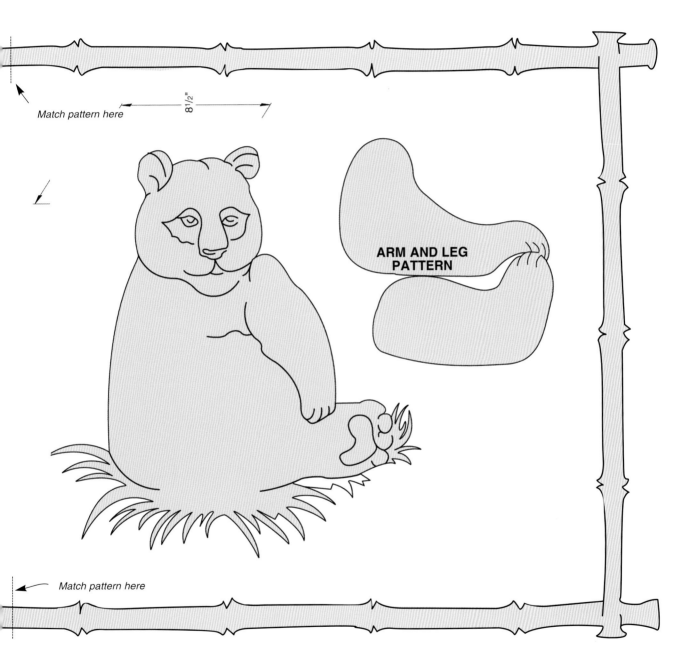

Match pattern here

8 1/2"

ARM AND LEG
PATTERN

Match pattern here

Playful Garden Markers

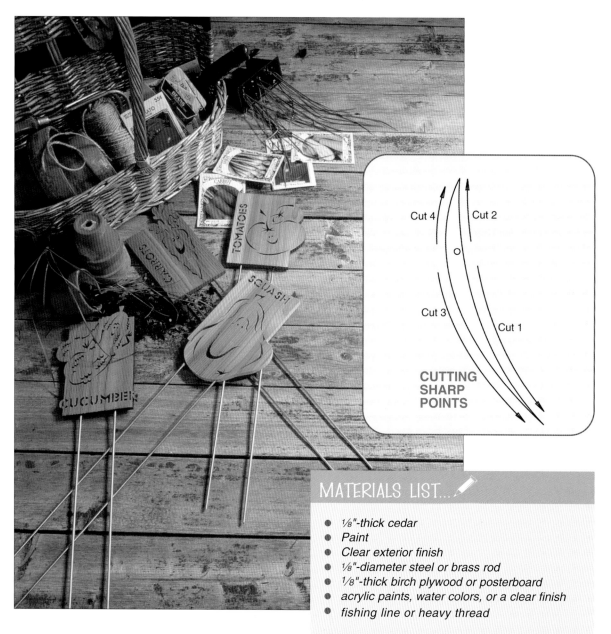

Cut 4

Cut 2

Cut 3

Cut 1

CUTTING SHARP POINTS

MATERIALS LIST...✎

- *⅛"-thick cedar*
- *Paint*
- *Clear exterior finish*
- *⅛"-diameter steel or brass rod*
- *⅛"-thick birch plywood or posterboard*
- *acrylic paints, water colors, or a clear finish*
- *fishing line or heavy thread*

NOTE: *The patterns for this project are shown at full size (100%).*

Painting the garden markers.

FULL-SIZED PLAYFUL GARDEN MARKERS continued

FULL-SIZED PLAYFUL GARDEN MARKERS continued

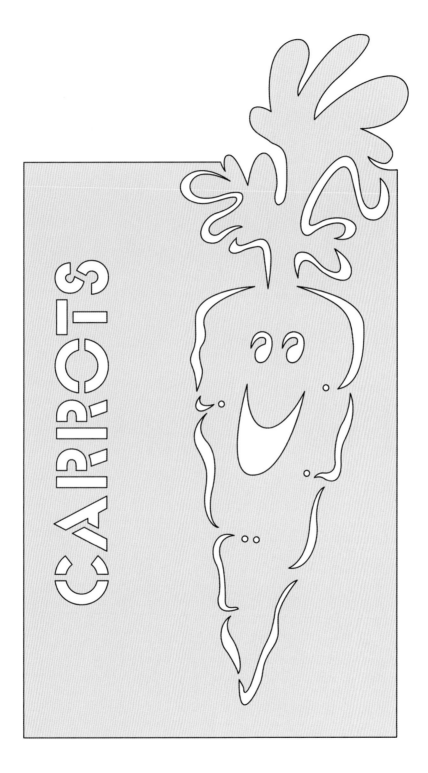

FULL-SIZED PLAYFUL GARDEN MARKERS continued

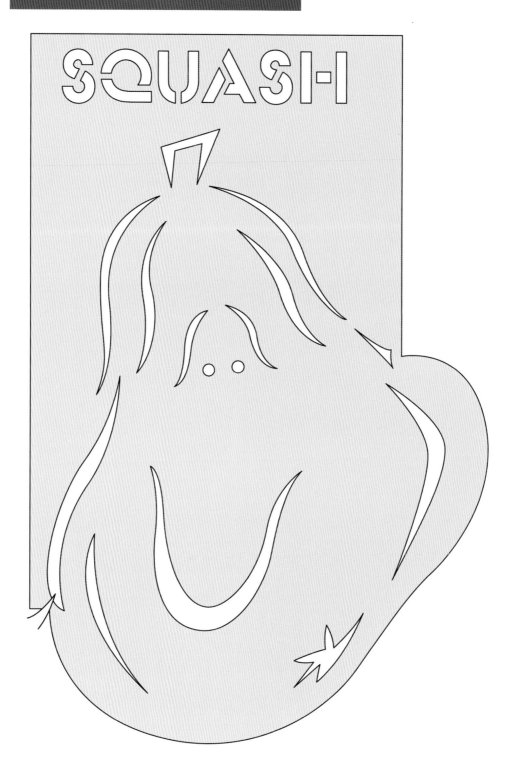

Snowflakes for Fun

This pattern is designed to be cut from ⅛" stock. It can be enlarged and cut from thicker stock.

Ⓒ fits here

Ⓐ fits here

Ⓑ

Ⓒ fits here

Slide Ⓐ and Ⓑ together. Attach parts Ⓒ where shown. Secure the pieces with a drop of glue at each joint.

Make two for each snowflake.

Ⓒ

MATERIALS LIST...

- ⅛"-thick birch plywood
- Glue
- Paint
- Glitter
- Monofilament fishing line

NOTE: The patterns for this project are shown at full size (100%.)

Swans Silhouette

MATERIALS LIST...

- ⅛"-thick birch plywood
- Clear finish
- ⅛"-thick birch plywood or posterboard
- acrylic paints, water colors, or a clear finish
- fishing line or heavy thread

NOTE: The patterns for this project are shown at full size (100%.)

Great American Skylines

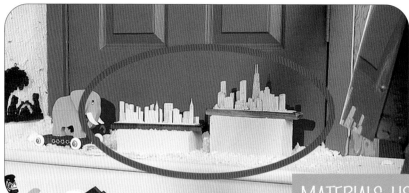

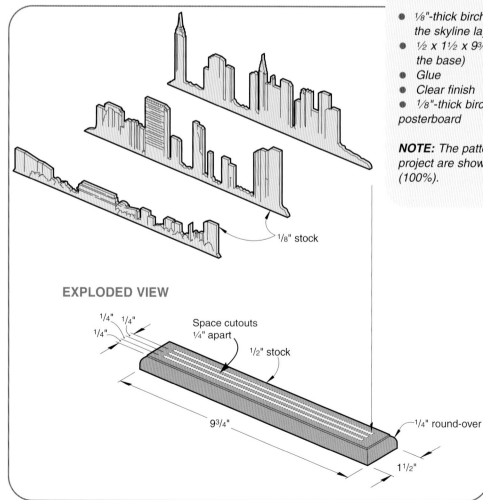

MATERIALS LIST...

- ⅛"-thick birch plywood (for the skyline layers)
- ½ x 1½ x 9¾" walnut (for the base)
- Glue
- Clear finish
- ⅛"-thick birch plywood or posterboard

NOTE: The patterns for this project are shown at full size (100%).

⅛" stock

EXPLODED VIEW

¼"   ¼"
¼"

Space cutouts ¼" apart

½" stock

9¾"

¼" round-over

1½"

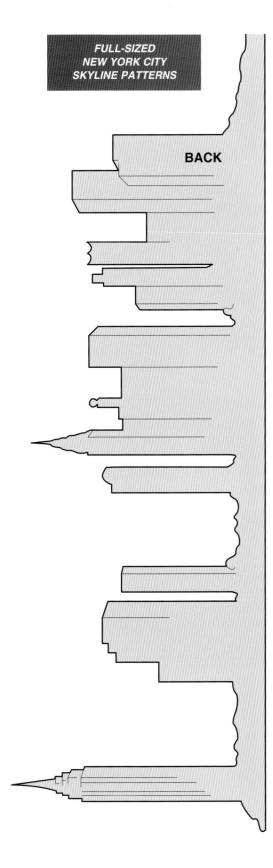

**FULL-SIZED
NEW YORK CITY
SKYLINE PATTERNS**

BACK

NEW YORK CITY

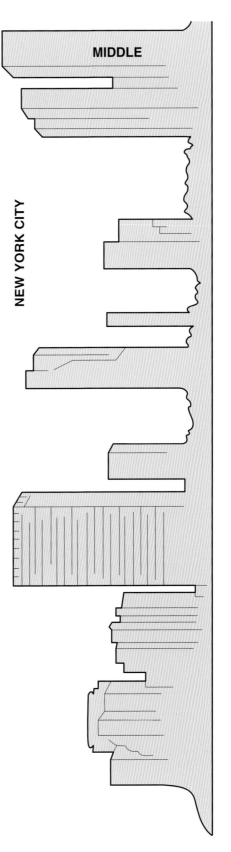

MIDDLE

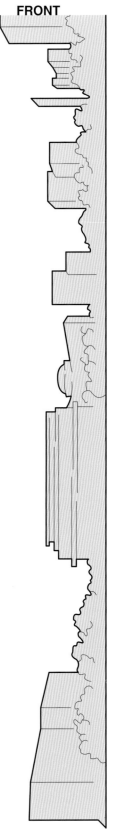

FRONT

FRONT

**CHICAGO FULL-SIZED
SKYLINE PATTERNS**

MIDDLE

CHICAGO

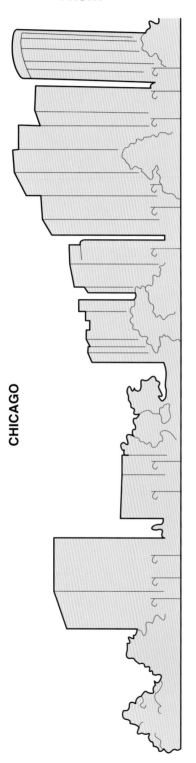

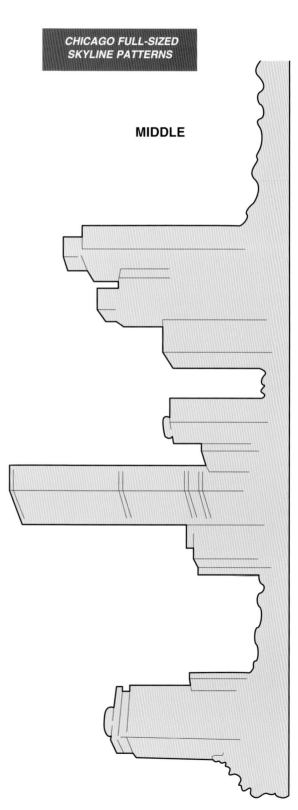

BACK

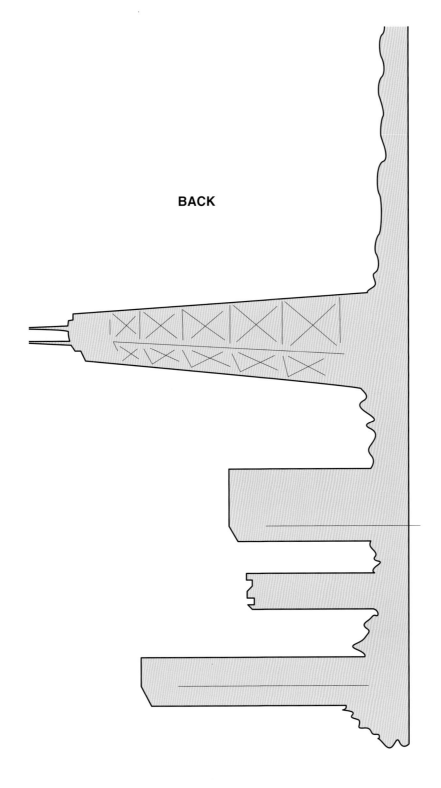

Angels Silhouette

MATERIALS LIST...

- ⅛"-thick birch plywood
- Clear finish

NOTE: The pattern for this project is shown at full size (100%).

Quail Country

MATERIALS LIST....

- ¼"-thick birch plywood
- ¾"-thick oak
- 1"-diameter dowels
- Glue
- Screws
- Stain
- Clear finish
- Rice paper
- Glass

NOTE: The pattern for this project is shown at full size (100%).

FULL-SIZED PATTERN

Cut out background
with a #2R blade.

(A)

Saw detail lines
with a #0 spiral blade.

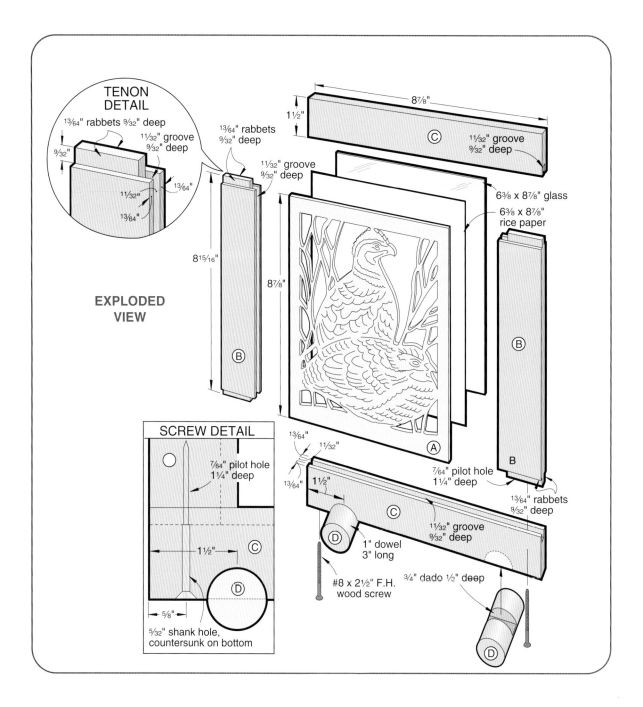

TENON
DETAIL

$^{13}/_{64}$" rabbets $^9/_{32}$" deep

$^{11}/_{32}$" groove
$^9/_{32}$" deep

$^9/_{32}$"

$^{11}/_{32}$"

$^{13}/_{64}$"

$^{13}/_{64}$"

EXPLODED
VIEW

$^{13}/_{64}$" rabbets
$^9/_{32}$" deep

$^{11}/_{32}$" groove
$^9/_{32}$" deep

$8^{15}/_{16}$"

$8^7/_8$"

Ⓑ

Ⓒ

$8^7/_8$"

$1^1/_2$"

$^{11}/_{32}$" groove
$^9/_{32}$" deep

$6^3/_8$ x $8^7/_8$" glass

$6^3/_8$ x $8^7/_8$"
rice paper

Ⓐ

Ⓑ

B

$^7/_{64}$" pilot hole
$1^1/_4$" deep

$^{13}/_{64}$" rabbets
$^9/_{32}$" deep

SCREW DETAIL

$^7/_{64}$" pilot hole
$1^1/_4$" deep

$1^1/_2$"

Ⓒ

Ⓓ

$^5/_8$"

$^5/_{32}$" shank hole,
countersunk on bottom

$^{13}/_{64}$"

$^{11}/_{32}$"

$^{13}/_{64}$"

$1^1/_2$"

Ⓒ

Ⓓ

1" dowel
3" long

#8 x $2^1/_2$" F.H.
wood screw

$^{11}/_{32}$" groove
$^9/_{32}$" deep

$^3/_4$" dado $^1/_2$" deep

Ⓓ

Advanced Patterns

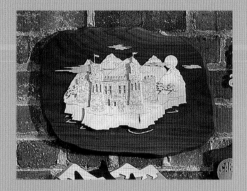

9

Picture-Perfect Patterns

Scrollsaw professionals pride themselves on the number of inside cuts
required on a pattern—the more the
better! They also like to challenge their
control with narrow cutouts between
millimeters of wood. If you enjoy these
things, too, you'll find the patterns in this
chaper right up your alley.

Castle on a Cliff

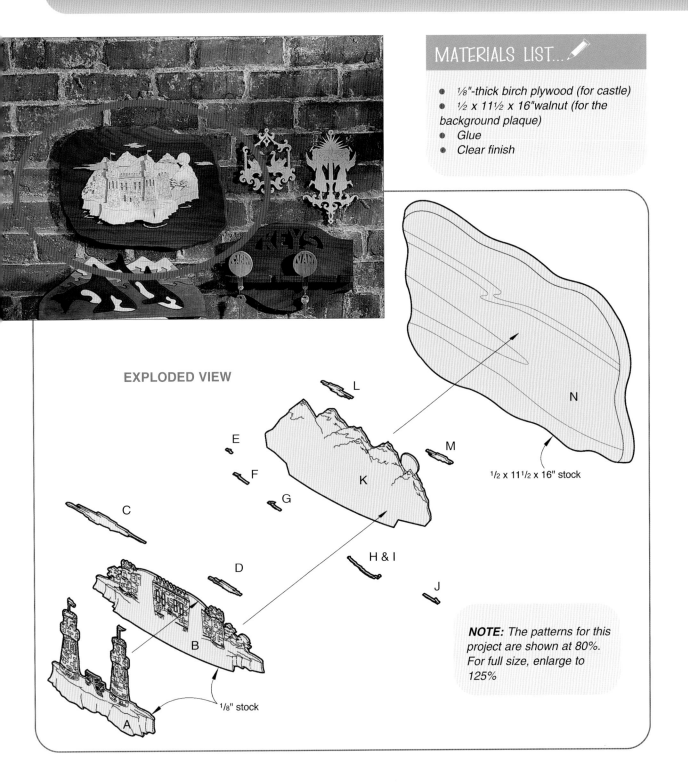

MATERIALS LIST...

- ⅛"-thick birch plywood (for castle)
- ½ x 11½ x 16"walnut (for the background plaque)
- Glue
- Clear finish

EXPLODED VIEW

N

½ x 11½ x 16" stock

L

E

F

M

G

K

C

D

H & I

J

B

NOTE: The patterns for this project are shown at 80%. For full size, enlarge to 125%

⅛" stock

A

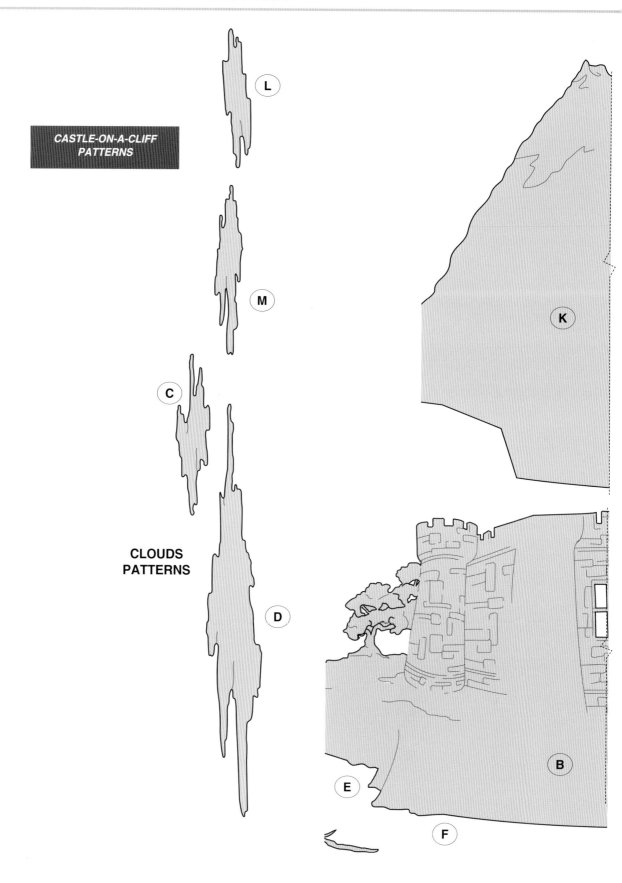

CASTLE-ON-A-CLIFF PATTERNS

CLOUDS PATTERNS

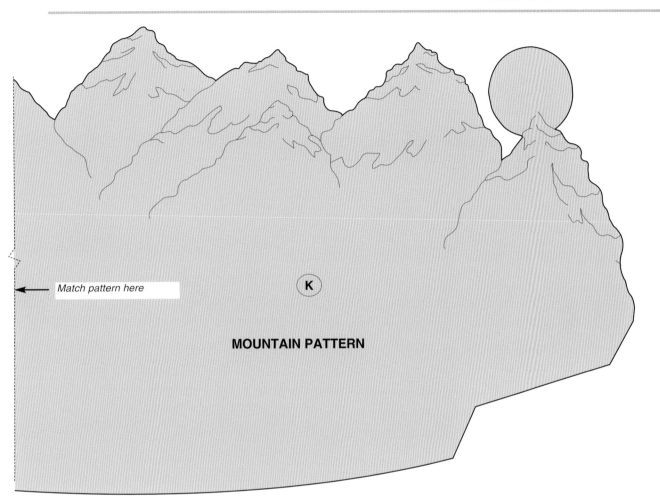

← *Match pattern here*

MOUNTAIN PATTERN

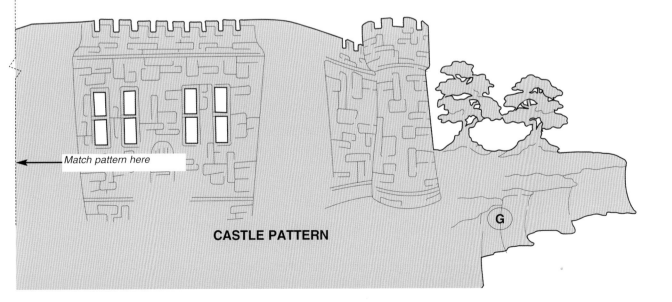

← *Match pattern here*

CASTLE PATTERN

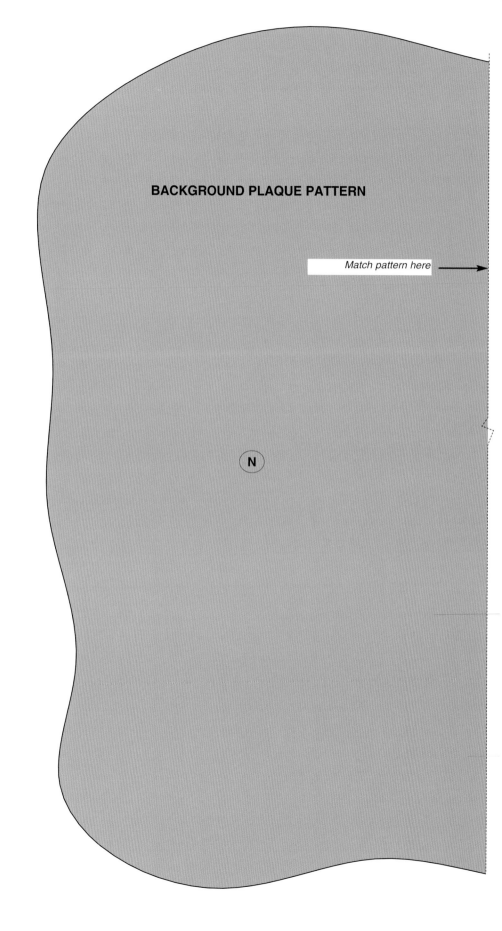

BACKGROUND PLAQUE PATTERN

Match pattern here

N

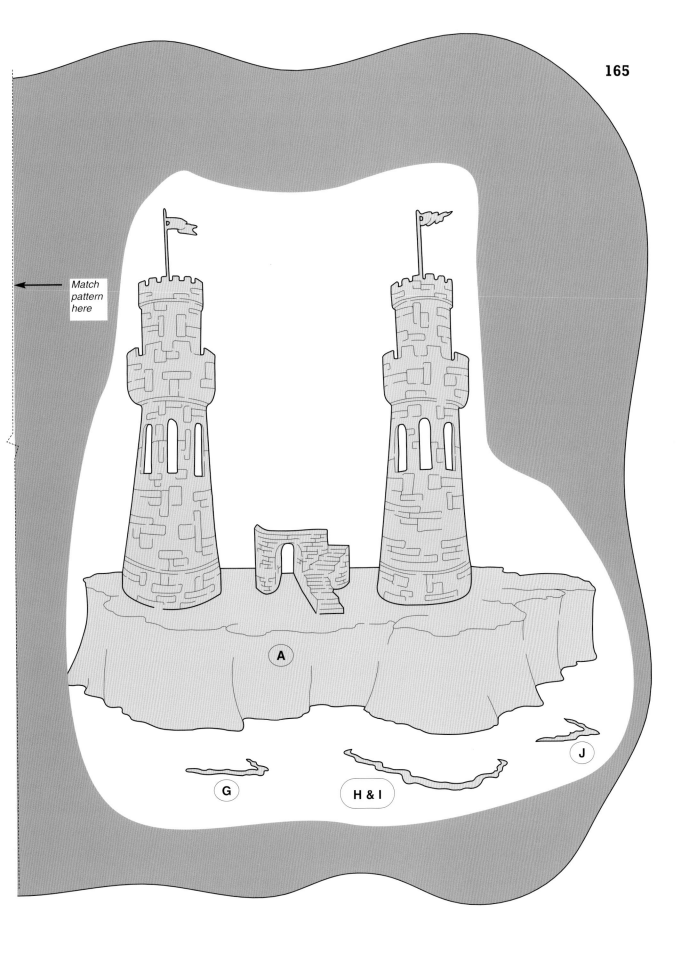

Match
pattern
here

A

G

H & I

J

Sitting Pretty Songbird

MATERIALS LIST...

- ⅛"-thick birch plywood
- ¾"-thick cedar (for the base)
- Glue
- Clear finish

NOTE: The patterns for this project are shown at full size (100%).

BASE PATTERN

FULL-SIZED SITTING PRETTY SONGBIRD PATTERNS

EXPLODED VIEW

1/8" stock

Midnight Visit and Campfire Cooking Plaques

Match pattern here →

**FULL-SIZED MIDNIGHT
VISIT PATTERN**

**FULL-SIZED CAMPFIRE
COOKING PATTERN**

1/8" hanging
hole on back

Brilliant Birds

MATERIALS LIST... ✏

- ¾ × 5¼ × 18"-thick poplar or pine (for scarlet macaw puzzle)
- ¾ × 4½ × 7"-thick poplar or pine (for pelican)
- Aniline dyes (or thinned acrylic paints)
- Glue
- Screws

NOTE: The patterns for this project are shown at 85%. For full size, enlarge to 118%.

These parrot and pelican puzzles aren't just play-things; they are colorful, artistic pieces that can be proudly displayed.

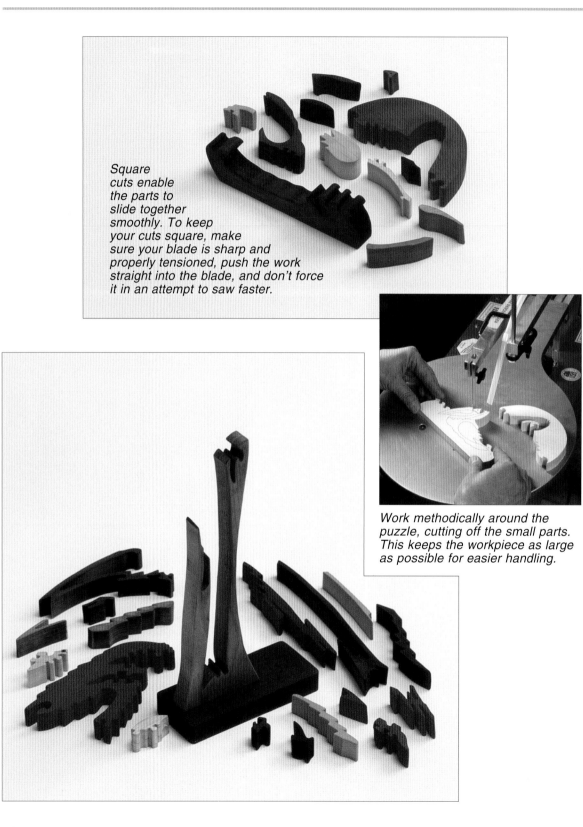

Square cuts enable the parts to slide together smoothly. To keep your cuts square, make sure your blade is sharp and properly tensioned, push the work straight into the blade, and don't force it in an attempt to saw faster.

Work methodically around the puzzle, cutting off the small parts. This keeps the workpiece as large as possible for easier handling.

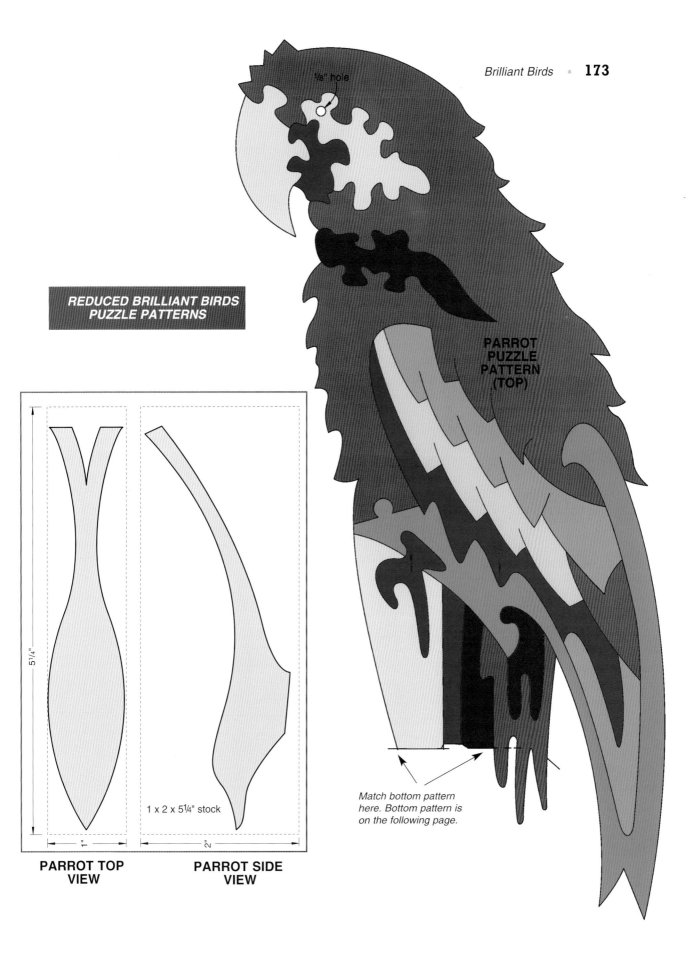

⅛" hole

**REDUCED BRILLIANT BIRDS
PUZZLE PATTERNS**

**PARROT
PUZZLE
PATTERN
(TOP)**

5¼"

1 x 2 x 5¼" stock

1"

2"

**PARROT TOP
VIEW**

**PARROT SIDE
VIEW**

*Match bottom pattern
here. Bottom pattern is
on the following page.*

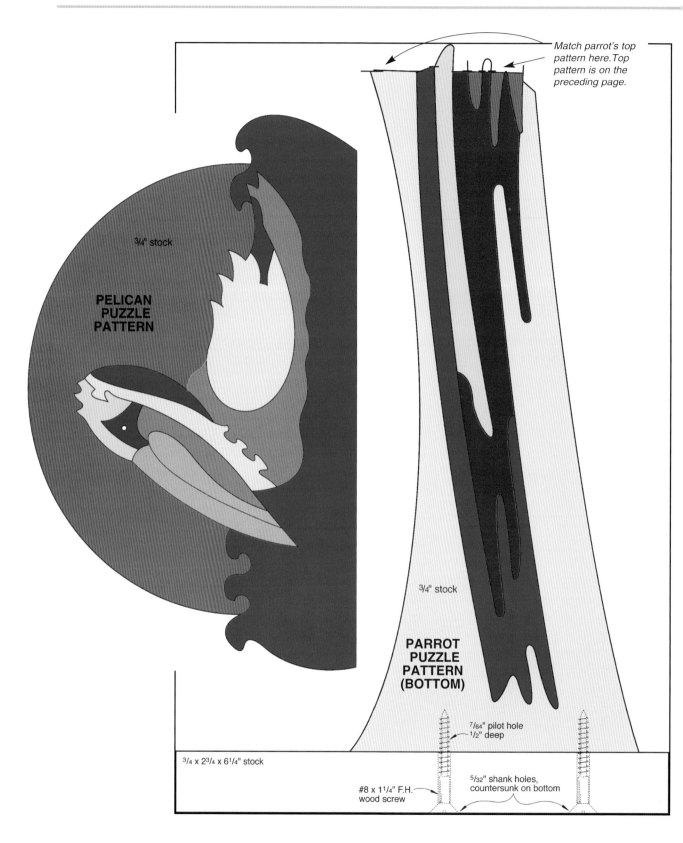

3/4" stock

PELICAN PUZZLE PATTERN

Match parrot's top pattern here. Top pattern is on the preceding page.

3/4" stock

PARROT PUZZLE PATTERN (BOTTOM)

$^7/_{64}$" pilot hole
$^1/_2$" deep

$^5/_{32}$" shank holes, countersunk on bottom

#8 x 1$^1/_4$" F.H. wood screw

$^3/_4$ x 2$^3/_4$ x 6$^1/_4$" stock

10

Fretwork Fantasies

Previous chapters barely touched on the subject of fretwork, the parlor pastime of days gone by. Gathered in this chapter, though, are some traditional fretwork projects to keep you busy, along with a winsome shelf with a seaside twist.

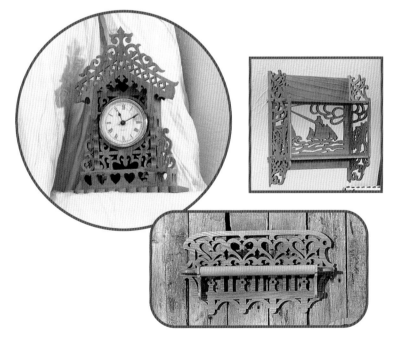

Cottage Clock

MATERIALS LIST...

- ⅜"-, ¼"-, and ⅛"-thick cherry or other hardwood
- Glue
- Clear finish
- Quartz clock movement

NOTE: The patterns for this project are shown at full size (100%).

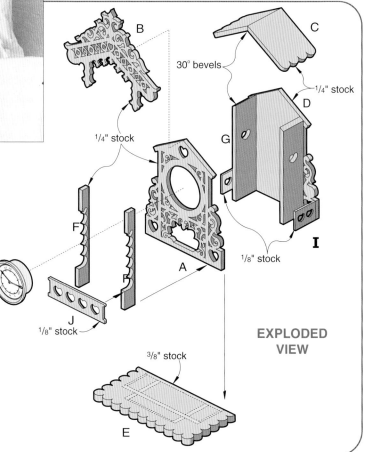

30° bevels

¼" stock

¼" stock

¼" stock

⅛" stock

⅛" stock

B

C

D

G

I

F

A

J

E

⅛" stock

⅜" stock

EXPLODED VIEW

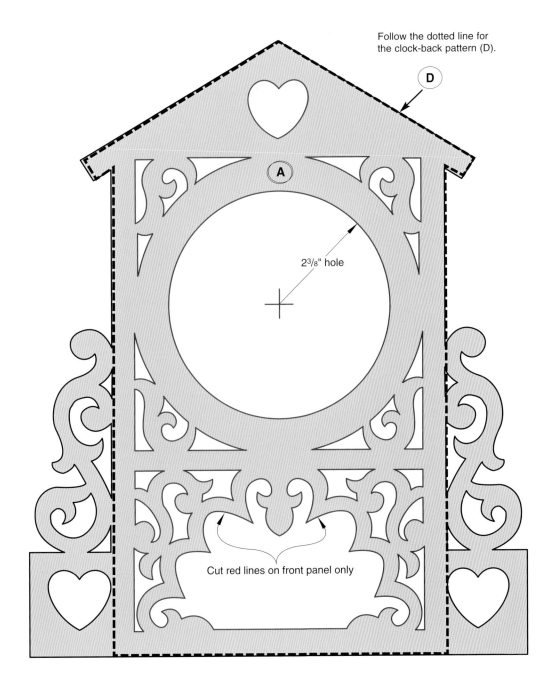

Follow the dotted line for
the clock-back pattern (D).

D

A

$2^3/_8$" hole

Cut red lines on front panel only

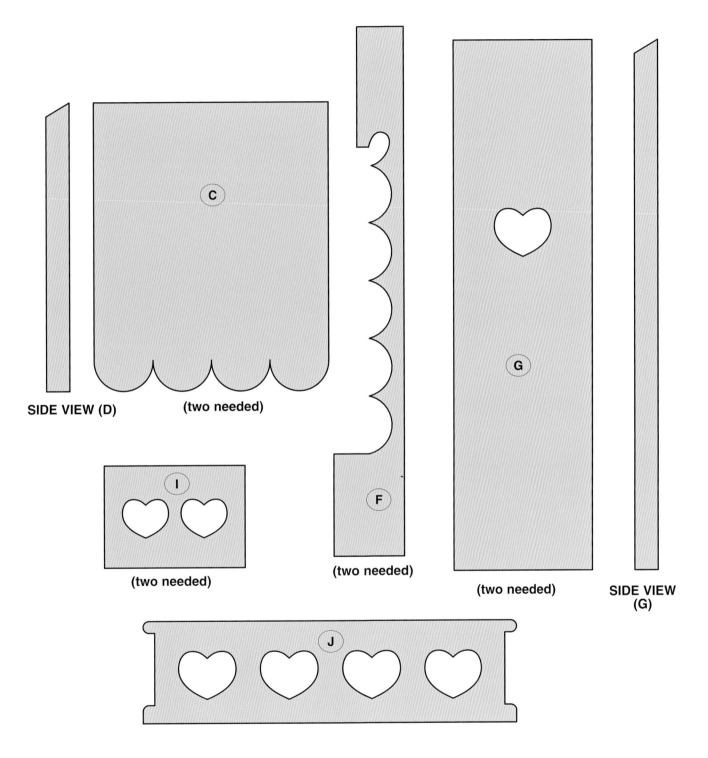

SIDE VIEW (D)

C

(two needed)

I

(two needed)

F

(two needed)

G

(two needed)

**SIDE VIEW
(G)**

J

Victorian Bathroom Accessories

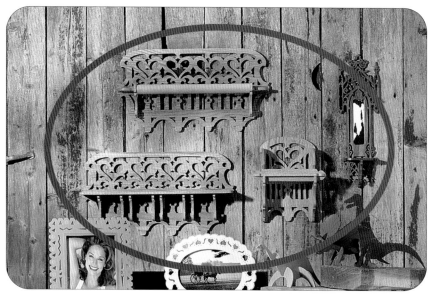

These Victorian fretwork bathroom accessories include a towel bar, shelf, and a posh paper holder.

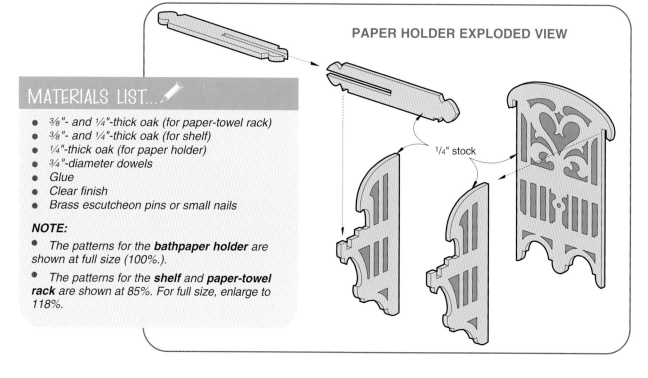

PAPER HOLDER EXPLODED VIEW

¹/₄" stock

MATERIALS LIST...

- ³/₈"- and ¹/₄"-thick oak (for paper-towel rack)
- ³/₈"- and ¹/₄"-thick oak (for shelf)
- ¹/₄"-thick oak (for paper holder)
- ³/₄"-diameter dowels
- Glue
- Clear finish
- Brass escutcheon pins or small nails

NOTE:

• The patterns for the **bathpaper holder** are shown at full size (100%.).

• The patterns for the **shelf** and **paper-towel rack** are shown at 85%. For full size, enlarge to 118%.

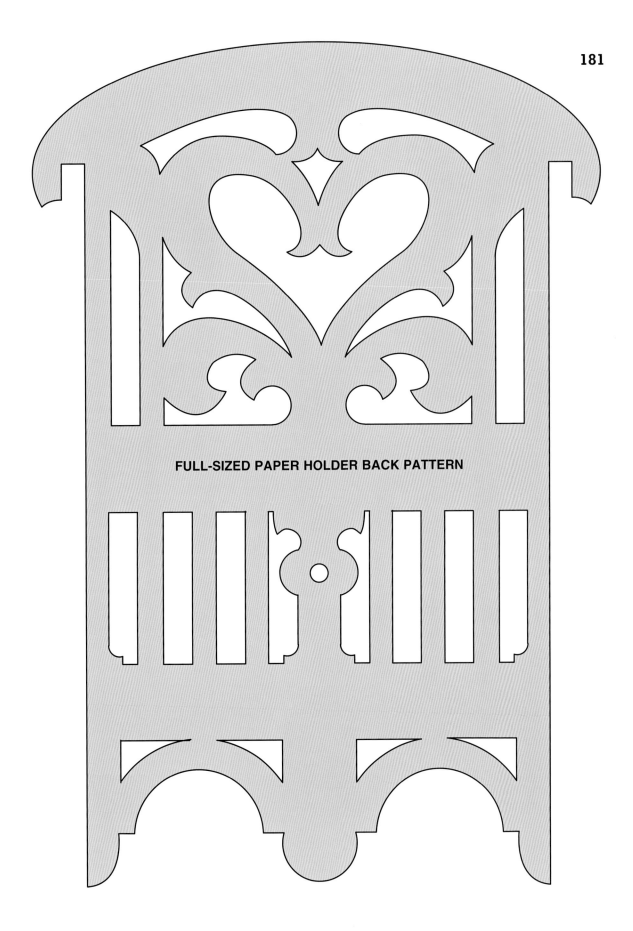

FULL-SIZED PAPER HOLDER BACK PATTERN

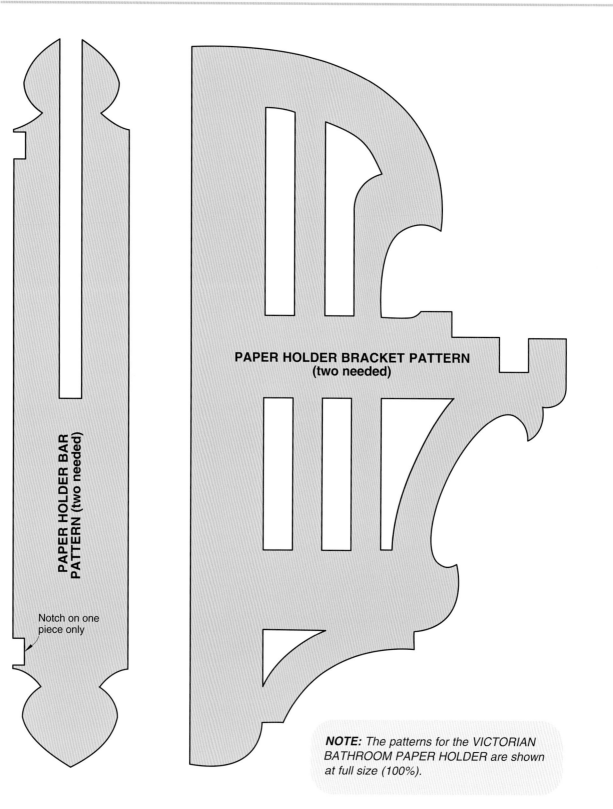

PAPER HOLDER BRACKET PATTERN
(two needed)

**PAPER HOLDER BAR
PATTERN (two needed)**

Notch on one
piece only

NOTE: *The patterns for the VICTORIAN
BATHROOM PAPER HOLDER are shown
at full size (100%).*

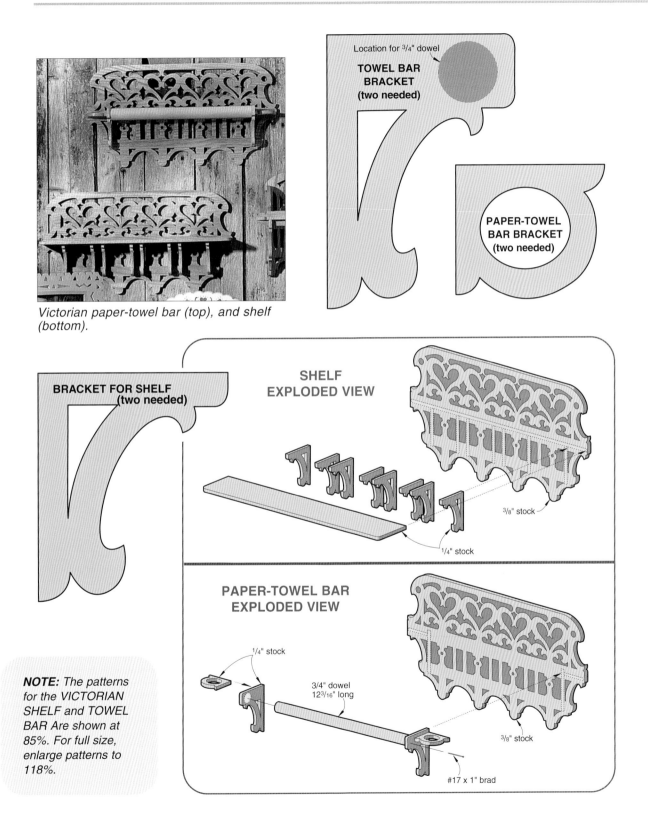

Victorian paper-towel bar (top), and shelf (bottom).

TOWEL BAR BRACKET (two needed)
Location for ³/₄" dowel

PAPER-TOWEL BAR BRACKET (two needed)

BRACKET FOR SHELF (two needed)

SHELF EXPLODED VIEW

³/₈" stock

¹/₄" stock

PAPER-TOWEL BAR EXPLODED VIEW

¹/₄" stock

³/₄" dowel 12³/₁₆" long

³/₈" stock

#17 x 1" brad

NOTE: The patterns for the VICTORIAN SHELF and TOWEL BAR Are shown at 85%. For full size, enlarge patterns to 118%.

VICTORIAN SHELF -

Match pattern here ⟶

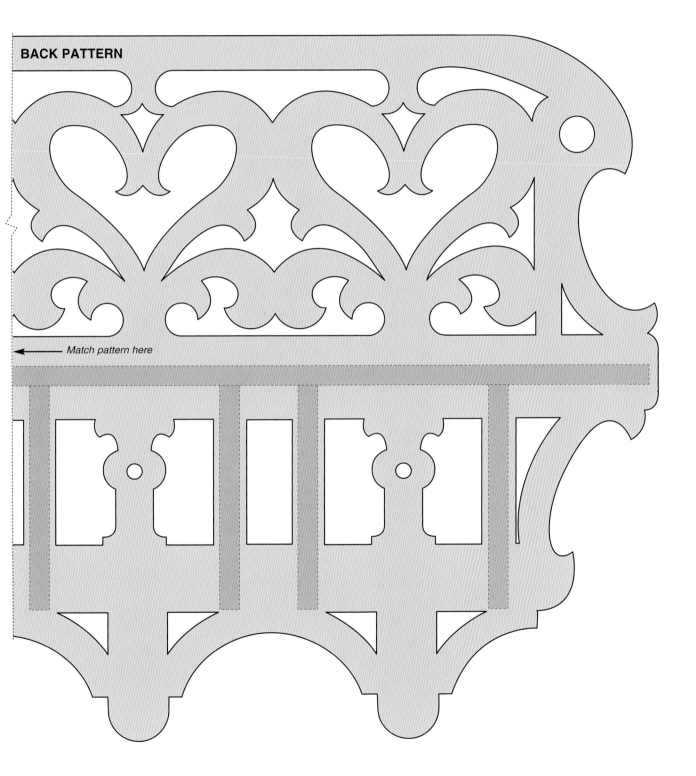

BACK PATTERN

← Match pattern here

Coastal Curio Shelf

Match pattern here ⟶

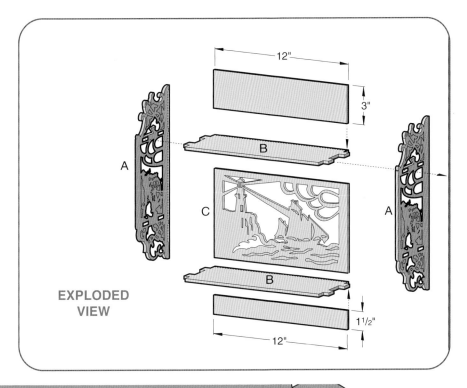

EXPLODED
VIEW

SIDE PATTERN (two needed)

(A)

**REDUCED
COASTAL
CURIO SHELF
PATTERNS**
continued

Match pattern here ⟶

SHELF PATTERN (two needed)

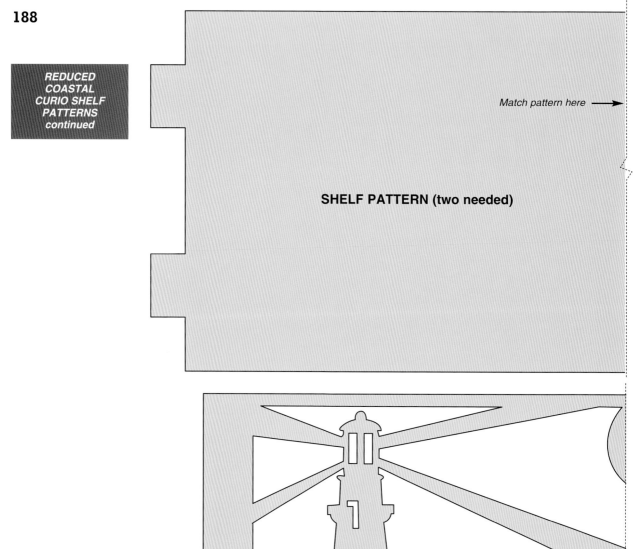

Match pattern here ⟶

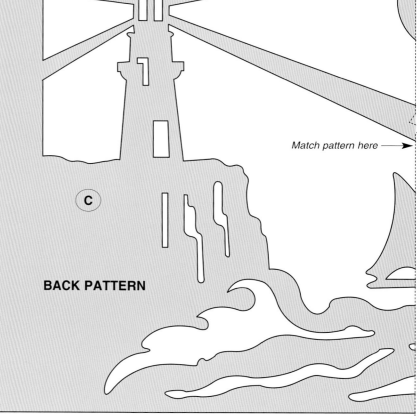

Ⓒ

BACK PATTERN

189

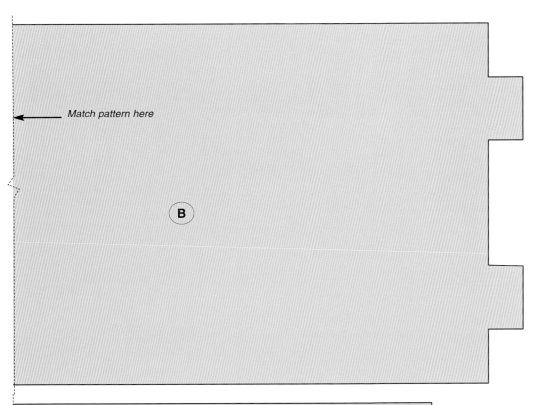

Match pattern here

B

Match pattern here

Index

Credits

Special thanks to the following people or companies for their contributions:

Christine Anderson, *for designing the Picture-Perfect Jungle Hut*

David Ashe, *for designing the Dandy Desk Trays, the Key-Clutter Cutter, and the Salad Servers with Drip Catcher*

Marty Baldwin, *for providing photography for the Music-Box Manger, One Fishy Puzzle, Reindeer in Flight and the Tabletop Reindeer*

Sue Banker, *for designing the Garden Markers*

Alfred Bavart, *for designing the Coastal Curio Shelf and the Cowboy Curio Shelf*

The Berry Basket, for designing the Music-Box Manger

Dick Boelman, *for designing the Cottage Clock, the Fretwork Hamper, the Tulip Time Desk Box, and the Victorian Bathroom Accessories*

Nancy Burgan, *for designing the Castle on a Cliff, the Cat-and-Dog Picture Frame, the Great American Skylines, the Picture-Perfect Panda, the Sitting Pretty Songbird, and the Towering Timepiece*

James Downing, *for providing drawings for the Music-Box Manger and designing the Old Oaken Clock*

Kim Downing, *for providing drawings for the Old Oaken Clock, the Safari Puzzle, the Season's Greetings Plate, the Towering Timepiece, and the Wetland Silhouette Clock*

Owen Duvall, *for providing text for the Bears Puzzle and One Fishy Puzzle*

Karl Ehlers, *for designing the Reindeer in Flight*

Lee Gatzke, *for designing the Tabletop Reindeer and the Bears Puzzle*

Russel Greenslade, *for designing One Fishy Puzzle*

Steve Grimes, *for designing Quail Country*

Carol Hayda, *for designing the Picture-Window Frame*

John Hetherington, *for providing photography for the Big Top, the Happy Holidays Tabletop Decoration, More Garden Markers, the Music-Box Manger, the Old Oaken Clock, Quail Country, the Safari Puzzle, the Season's Greetings Plate, the Wetland Silhouette Clock, and the Wonderful Whatnot Shelf*

Christi Lausly, *for designing the Big Top*

Brian Jensen, *for providing drawings for Kid's First Car, the Land and Sea Combo, the Little Buddy Bulldozer, and the Over-the-Rug Hauler*

Lorna Johnson, *for providing drawings for the Big Top, More Garden Markers, the Music-Box Manger, the Old Oaken Clock, Quail Country, and Reindeer in Flight*

Gunter Keil, *for designing the Dangling Dinosaurs*

King Au, *for providing photography for the Towering Timepiece*

Roxanne LeMoine, *for providing drawings for Quail Country, the Happy Holidays Tabletop Decoration, More Garden Markers, the Romping Reptiles, and the Wonderful Whatnot Shelf*

William Lewis, *for providing photography for One Fishy Puzzle*

Rick Longabaugh, *for designing the Music-Box Manger*

Angie Medici, *for designing the Hair-Care Appliance Holder, the Lace-Edged Memento Box, and the Top-of-the-Morning Toast Rack*

Mike Mittermeyer, *for designing and providing illustrations for Reindeer in Flight*

Nelson Designs, *for designing the Wonderful Whatnot Shelf*

Paula Nelson, *for designing More Garden Markers*

Judy Gale Roberts, *for designing and providing drawings for the Season's Greetings Plate*

Kim and **Rob Russell**, *for designing the Happy Holidays Tabletop Decoration*

Scroller, *for designing the Angels Silhouette, the Colorful Kachina, and the Swans Silhouette*

Dianne Shannon, *for designing the Great Puzzle Fish*

Jan Svec, *for providing text for the Reindeer in Flight and Quail Country*

Bill Zaun, *for designing the Breakfast Blooms Napkin Holder, the Desktop Dolphin, the Prehistoric Puzzlers, the Tricky Clown Clock, the Wetland Silhouette Clock*

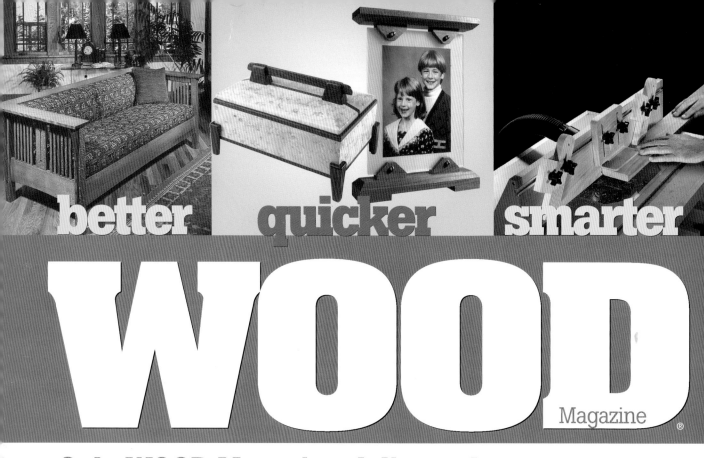